# Essays in International Refugee Law

Essays in International Refugee Law Copyright © Azra Hodzic, Stella Ngugi, Robert W. Reed and M. Siraj Sait. 2018 All Rights Reserved.

All rights reserved. No part of this book may be reproduced in any form or by any electronic or mechanical means including information storage and retrieval systems, without permission in writing from the author. The only exception is by a reviewer, who may quote short excerpts in a review.

Cover image is a photo taken by the U.S. Department of State of the Za'atri camp in Jordan for Syrian refugees

Printed in the United Kingdom

First Published: Nov 2016
Second edition Nov 2018

First edition: ISBN-13 978-3-7418712-2-1
Second edition: ISBN 13 978-1-9733485-8-0

# Contributors

**Azra Hodzic**, School of Law and Business, University of East London Azra holds a LLM in International Law and Criminal Justice from the University of East London, and a BA International Relations from the Høgskolen i Lillehammer (Lillehammer University College). Azra has experience working in the Western Balkans on several aspects of peacebuilding, such as post-conflict reconstruction, program support for the rule of law, forced migration issues, EU-integration and development projects. Azra has also worked with NGOs such as Group 484, and the Helsinki Committee for Rights in Serbia, she has also worked in the Norwegian Embassy in Belgrade. Azra's area of focus is small state political relations and Norwegian foreign policy.

**Stella Ngugi**, School of Law and Business, University of East London Bachelor of laws(LLB); BA International Relations; Advocate of the High Court of Kenya; LLM International Law & International Relations; passionate about refugee affairs and keen to contribute to the enhancement of the prominence of International Refugee Law in the internal and foreign policy considerations of governments.

**Robert W Reed**, School of Law and Business, University of East London Robert holds a LLM in International Law and Criminal Justice, MSc in Terrorism Studies, and a BA(hons) in Legal Studies from the University of East London and has worked for a number of NGOs working in educational provision for excluded groups of youths, or in generalist legal advice, he has also worked on a *pro bono* capacity to criminal appeals cases. Robert has served with HM Armed Forces as a Sapper in the Corps of Royal Engineers. His area of primary academic focus is International Law in regard to terrorism and refugees, and narratives in regard to radicalisation. Robert is currently a research assistant to the Deputy Vice-Chancellor of the University of East London, and the Communications Coordinator for the UEL Centre for Islamic Finance, Law and Communities (CIFLAC).

**M Siraj Sait**, School of Law and Business, University of East London Siraj is a graduate of University of Madras (India), University of London and Harvard Law School. His areas of expertise are human rights, gender and land/housing, refugee and post-conflict studies and Islamic law. A lawyer by training, he has held served several key posts such as State Prosecutor on Human Rights in India, and has been closely associated with several grassroots campaigns and NGOs, as a consultant for Minority Rights Group International and as a trustee of the Commonwealth Human Rights Initiative. Since 2006, he has been member of the International Advisory Board of the Global Land Tool Network www.gltn.net. He is also on the MTSIP Review Panel of UN-HABITAT and the World Bank's project evaluation committee. Siraj is currently the Director of the UEL Centre for Islamic Finance, Law and Communities (CIFLAC), and a Reader in Law at the School of Law and Business.

# Table Of Contents

| | |
|---|---|
| Editor's Foreword | 1 |
| Introduction | 16 |
| From Refugee Rights Principles To Rights Based Approaches | 25 |
| **M. Siraj Sait** | |
| The Battle For Ownership And The Future Of Refugee Law | 49 |
| **M. Siraj Sait** | |
| An Examination Of The Transformation Of The Border To Define States Obligations In Refugee Protection | 74 |
| **Stella Ngugi** | |
| Resolving Disputes Of Land As A Peacebuilding Project: Is the Bosnian model applicable to other post-conflict societies? | 92 |
| **Azra Hodzic** | |
| The Securitisation Of The UK: Refugees perceived as potential terrorists and their resulting treatment within the international legal framework by the UK | 117 |
| **Robert W. Reed** | |
| Index | 141 |

# Editor's Foreword

## Robert W. Reed

Started in mid-2015, this book is a collection of papers which have been written based on personal perspective within the writer's experience of migration due to persecution. For some this may be direct, for others it is the effects of migration, but always there is a consideration of the secondary effect of migration by those who have fled persecution - the policies of countries who provide protection, and those who try to avoid that obligation, or simply the problems associated by the title ownership of things left behind by the refugees.

Migration has become an increasingly contentious issue, with politicians using the issue of migration to win votes[1], or at least prevent the opposition parties from gaining any support. The media often uses the term 'illegal immigrant', a term which is both deliberately divisive and erroneous[2], to mean a range of people who have fled several backgrounds, much of which would entitle them to protection in law by the states that they have fled to.

When many people talk about refugees the conversation is typically used to mean several things which are generally confused and used by the uninitiated, interchangeably. This is often done in popular discourse by the media to illicit a response in the reader; *De facto* refugees, *De jure* refugees, People in refugee-like situations, people who have Humanitarian protection, Internally Displaced Persons, Asylum seekers, and the most divisive of all, Economic migrants.

*De facto* refugees are probably the least contentious for anyone other than the state which they are fleeing, they are the people who have left their state because of persecution of some kind and are unwilling to avail themselves of the protection of the state. This is the least contentious because it is a matter of fact, not law; *De facto*

---

[1] Oliver Wright, 'Eu Referendum: Nigel Farage's Anti-Migrant Poster Like 1930s Fascist Propaganda, Says George Osborne' (*The Independent*, 2016) <www.independent.co.uk/news/uk/politics/eu-referendum-poster-nigel-farage-polls-michael-gove-a7089946.html> accessed 25/11/2016

[2] The 1951 Convention Relating to the Status of Refugees and the 1967 Protocol, Article 32 (2)

refugees do not necessarily accrue any rights other than the goodwill of the state which they have fled to.

*De Jure* refugees are the refugees which have had their claim to asylum processed and have been granted full protection of the state into which they have fled; de jure refugees are afforded the full range of obligations, protections and rights of the state as are applicable to the full citizens of that state. The definition of who is a refugee comes from the 1951 United Nations Convention Relating to the Status of Refugees, and the 1967 Protocol Relating to the Status of Refugees which states that a refugee is an individual who:

> *"owing to a well-founded fear of being persecuted for reasons of race, religion, nationality, membership of a particular social group or political opinion, is outside the country of his nationality, and is unable or — unwilling to avail himself of the protection of that country."*

'People in refugee-like situations' are exactly that, they have fled their state to another due to a fear of persecution but are not recognised as such due to inaction or inability by the state, this category is applicable to groups such as the Bedouin in parts of the Middle East, and the Burmese in parts of Southeast Asia. These groups are in a grey area between refugee and being ignored by the state in which they are in does not recognise them as any of the other categories but does not request that they leave the country they are in.

The last two categories are the two most contentious[3], and the term is often as a pejorative against refugees in general. The first of these last two categories is 'economic migrant', this person is someone whose reason for leaving their country of citizenship is purely one of economic means; they have migrated merely to improve their standard of living.

An asylum seeker is a person who has potentially left their country of origin because of a well-founded fear of being persecuted and is unable, or unwilling to seek the protection of their country of origin, but they have not yet had their claim to refugee protection assessed; they are in-between the *de facto* and *de jure* definitions of refugee. Those who have failed to be granted refugee protected status

---

[3] Lizzie Dearden, 'How Economic Migrants Become Refugees as They Seek a New Life' 2016) <www.independent.co.uk/news/world/europe/refugees-economic-migrants-europe-crisis-difference-middle-east-africa-libya-mediterranean-sea-a7432516.html> accessed 25/11/2016 ; Editorial, 'Dentists Condemn Call for Child Migrants' Teeth to Be Tested' (*BBC*, 2016) <www.bbc.co.uk/news/uk-37700074> accessed 19/10/2016

can, at the discretion of the protecting state, be given 'Humanitarian protected' status, this allows the claimant to remain in the state providing protection but does not give any rights aside those given in international law, such as a right to life, liberty, and security of person.

The last definition which this book is concerned with, is that of 'Internally Displaced Persons' or IDPs, this group of people would be considered for protection were it not for the fact that they have not left their country of origin, they are unable to obtain the protection of their state, however. This situation often happens in states which are in the process of internal conflict and the IDP population are in areas in which the state is unable to operate due to that conflict.

To help prevent variations in the application of the treaties and the implications of a state failing to apply the treaty, the treaty's custodian, the United Nations High Commissioner for Refugees (UNHCR) is charged with ensuring that the refugee's rights are protected in international law, they also have responsibility for the welfare of refugees living in the refugee camps – The United Nations Relief and Works Agency for Palestine Refugees in the Near East (UNRWA) has a similar function, but is confined to working with Palestine refugees in Jordan, Lebanon, Syria, the Gaza Strip and the West Bank; the work of UNRWA is beyond the scope of this book.

One of the most important, if not the most important principle of international law regarding the various categories of refugees supervised by the UNHCR, is the principle of *non-refoulement*, in basic terms the principle prohibits the return of someone who is a refugee to a country where they are likely to suffer persecution; however, the term goes further than this, encompassing those who may be entitled to refugee protection, by enforcing the rule against states in a blanket policy – every person who is seeking refugee protection must be assessed on their own merits, rather than that of a group.

The issue of a blanket policy may prove quite contentious for several reasons, in one direction the policy may be seen to encourage migrants of all categories going to certain countries, such as was argued by political commentators in both Germany[4] and Sweden[5], when they offered a blanket policy of accepting Syrian migrants[6].

---

[4] Alison Smale, 'Flooded with Migrants, Germany Struggles to Integrate Them' (*The New York Times*, 2016) <www.nytimes.com/2016/04/28/world/europe/germany-migrants-struggles-to-integrate.html?_r=0> accessed 25/11/2016

[5] Dan Harris and Jackie Jesko, 'Anti-Immigrant Protests Grow as Thousands of Refugees Flood Europe' (*ABC News*, 2015)
<http://abcnews.go.com/International/anti-immigrant-protests-grow-thousands-refugees-flood-europe/story?id=35888428> accessed 25/11/2016

[6] Allan Hall and John Lichfield, 'Germany Opens Its Gates: Berlin Says All Syrian

Conversely, a blanket policy which deliberately frustrates the ability for *de facto* refugees to seek asylum, such as in the case of Hungary[7] or Australia[8], can lead to the ire of many international organisations, as well as a varying number of their own population.

A blanket policy to accept migrants of a kind can be instituted for several reasons, but in general terms this will be done in the case of conflict; particularly, where it causes humanitarian effects in the surrounding countries. The policy to accept Syrian refugees was done in the light of many leaving the region to come to Europe, either being trafficked, or having left the refugee camps in the surrounding countries when they have been unable to obtain sufficient support, been unable to support themselves, or simply that they feel that they would have a better life opportunity with *de jure* refugee status.

The decision for a migrant to pick one country over many others where they can be determined by several factors: cultural affinity, the perception of fairness and rule of law, or merely that the migrant feels that they would be best able to create an opportunity for themselves[9]. This can also mean that they have a support network of likeminded diaspora, or even family members who can help them integrate into the country offering protection. The choice of country may not always be their own, however, and many migrants will have paid or been promised a 'new life' in the

---

Asylum-Seekers Are Welcome to Remain, as Britain Is Urged to Make a 'Similar Statement'' (*The Independent*, 2015) <www.independent.co.uk/news/world/europe/germany-opens-its-gates-berlin-says-all-syrian-asylum-seekers-are-welcome-to-remain-as-britain-is-10470062.html> accessed 25/11/2016

[7] Lizzie Dearden, 'Hungary Planning 'Massive' New Border Fence to Keep out Refugees as Pm Vows to 'Hold Them Back by Force'' (*The Independent*, 2016) <www.independent.co.uk/news/world/europe/hungary-massive-new-border-fence-to-keep-out-refugees-prime-minister-orban-turkey-eu-hold-them-back-a7212696.html> accessed 25/11/2016

[8] Andreas Schloenhardt 'To Deter, Detain and Deny : Protection of Onshore Asylum Seekers in Australia' (2002) 14(2-3) International journal of refugee law International journal of refugee law 302: ; Anthony Mughan and Pamela Paxton, 'Anti-Immigrant Sentiment, Policy Preferences and Populist Party Voting in Australia' (2006) 36(British Journal of Political Science 341:

[9] Lizzie Dearden, 'Majority of Refugees Arriving in Europe Never Wanted to Come to Continent' (*The Independent*, 2016) <www.independent.co.uk/news/world/europe/refugees-europe-never-wanted-to-come-libya-mediterranean-deaths-economic-migrants-torture-abuse-a7432066.html> accessed 25/11/2016 ; Dearden, 'How Economic Migrants Become Refugees as They Seek a New Life' ; Lucy Mayblin, *Asylum Seekers in Britain: Putting the Economic 'Pull Factor' in Context* (LSE 2016):

country by people attempting to exploit migrants, and these exploited people will be trafficked into slavery or prostitution.

Countries can be both net recipients of refugee migrants and concurrently being exporters of refugee migrants; this can occur when a country is divisive towards a group and the people belonging to that group feel unable to seek the protection of their country. This is more prevalent in countries with weaker recourse to the rule of law, and many countries within the continent of Africa acknowledge that fact and have gone beyond the provisions of the 1951 United Nations Convention Relating to the Status of Refugees, and the 1967 Protocol Relating to the Status of Refugees (CSR), by instituting a regional refugee convention, the 1969 Organization of African Unity (OAU), Convention Governing the Specific Aspects of Refugee Problems in Africa (OAU Convention of 1969). This convention widens the definition of who is entitled to refugee protection within the CSR:

> *"owing to external aggression, occupation, foreign domination, or events seriously disturbing the public order...is compelled to leave...to seek refuge in another place outside his country of origin or nationality."*

Europe has also gone some way to instituting a regional variation to the CSR with many the EU member states applying the 'Dublin' conventions; this treats the EU area as a single state, making the country which is the first port of entry to the EU to the migrant, the state which is obligated to process the asylum claim to refugee protection. This has not been without problems however; Greece has been so overwhelmed and under resourced that it is now unable to process migrants as the first port of entry effectively, and is considered as a breach of Article 3 of the European Convention on Human Rights based on being inhuman treatment, states are therefore unable to transfer migrants to Greece as the first port of entry under the Dublin III rules[10]. Several of the transit route states have applied the rules in a varying manner, with Italy attempting to document migrants for processing, but allowing their progress through the overwhelming numbers of migrants[11], and Hungary deliberately frustrating the progress of those attempting to enter the EU through the Balkans *en route* to Germany, Austria and the Northern EU states[12].

---

[10] *Mss V Belgium & Greece (2011)* (ECtHR)

[11] Ian Traynor, 'Italy Threatens to Give Schengen Visas to Migrants as Eu Ministers Meet' (*The Guardian*, 2015)
<https://www.theguardian.com/world/2015/jun/15/italy-threatens-to-give-schengen-visas-to-migrants-as-eu-dispute-deepens> accessed 25/11/2016 ;
Editorial, 'Eu Policy Pushes Refugees to Illegal Travel Routes' (*The New Arab*, 2015)
<https://www.alaraby.co.uk/english/politics/2015/6/22/eu-policy-pushes-refugees-to-illegal-travel-routes> accessed 25/11/2016

This variable application of the CSR and Dublin rules has led to a 'race to the bottom' in many of the EU states due to internal political movements; Denmark made a series of rhetorical statements and legislative provisions which were designed to transfer migrants to their neighbours, Sweden, who were accepting large numbers of Syrian migrants as a blanket policy[13]. Similar arguments were made in Norway and the United Kingdom based on the cultural aspect of providing for refugees being through money in these two countries; the good will of the population is based on the perception that refugees should be paid for and kept in other countries – 'at arm's length'[14]. In the United Kingdom, this perception of the deserving refugee versus the undeserving economic migrant narrative has led to large groups of migrants living in makeshift camps in France awaiting the opportunity to enter the UK irregularly[15].

The complex and obfuscated nature of international, regional and national refugee legislation has been seized upon by far-right groups and deliberately conflated with a number of other issues, such as the EU freedom of movement, to create a cadre of voters who have been disaffected by a stagnation in wages, and a rarity in state provision, coupled with a propensity for neoliberal executives to defer blame for policies to external actors, then these voters have used their democratic voice at the behest of the far-right and right wing political actors, which have led to the 'Brexit' referendum result, and the election of Donald J Trump[16].

---

[12] Patrick Kingsley, 'Refugees Enter Croatia from Serbia after Hungary Blocks Border' (*The Guardian*, 2015) <https://www.theguardian.com/world/2015/sep/16/refugees-enter-croatia-from-serbia-after-hungary-blocks-border> accessed 25/11/2016

[13] Sasha Abramsky, 'If Sweden and Denmark Are So Progressive, Why Did They Close Their Doors to Refugees?' (*The Nation*, 2016) <https://www.thenation.com/article/if-sweden-and-denmark-are-so-progressive-why-did-they-close-their-doors-to-refugees/> accessed 25/11/2016

[14] Chiara Palazzo, 'Norway Offers to Pay Asylum Seekers £1000 Bonus to Leave the Country' (*The Telegraph*, 2016) <www.telegraph.co.uk/news/2016/04/26/norway-to-pay-asylum-seekers-extra-money-to-leave/> accessed 25/11/2016 ; Editorial, 'Migrant Crisis: What Is the Uk Doing to Help?' (*BBC*, 2016) <http://www.bbc.co.uk/news/uk-34139960> accessed 25/11/2016

[15] Andy Jones, 'I've Seen First Hand How Easily Our Asylum System Can Be Abused – and There's No Real Way to Stop It' (*The Telegraph*, 2016) <www.telegraph.co.uk/news/2016/10/30/ive-seen-first-hand-how-easily-our-asylum-system-can-be-abused/> accessed 25/11/2016

[16] James Chater, 'What Are the Consequences of Brexit for the Refugee Crisis?' (*The New Statesman*, 2016) <www.newstatesman.com/politics/uk/2016/06/what-are-consequences-brexit-refugee-crisis> accessed 25/11/2016 ; Lauren Gambino and Patrick Kingsley, 'Refugees in Us Nervously Await Trump Presidency after Campaign Rhetoric' (*The Guardian*, 2016) <https://www.theguardian.com/us-news/2016/nov/24/refugees-in-us-trump-administration-syria> accessed

The negative narrative is a very persuasive argument and has been deliberately used by both political actors and the right of centre press; in the EU, particularly the newspapers in the UK[17]. This has led to the widespread belief that migrants are a burden on the country and that it is draining the resources to accept migrants[18]. One argument surrounds the issue of security, particularly about terrorist insurgents and war criminals, and the state goes to great lengths to ascertain the involvement, if any, of anyone seeking refugee protection from a state who has been involved in conflict[19]. However, in some cases this has been tolerated or even encouraged, with some of the Afghan *mujahedeen* in Pakistan being armed by China, France, Pakistan, Saudi Arabia, the United Kingdom and the United States, to fight the Soviet occupation of Afghanistan (with Germany unable to arm but in support)[20] – Some of the *mujahedeen* were citizens of other countries, and returned to those countries following the occupation, further confusing the matter regarding security issues[21].

The perceived burden extends to the issue of welfare provision and services offered to refugees, with a widespread belief that refugees are entitled to far more help from the state than is available to the citizens of that state; however, even in countries with a well-established welfare benefits system, this is not the case, with housing being provided on an equivalent basis for refugees as for citizens and the pecuniary benefits being offered on the same basis as a citizen of the UK being placed in equivalent position[22] – this is a requirement of the CSR. Unfortunately, like

---

25/11/2016 ; Michael Jacobs and Mariana Mazzucato, *The Brexit-Trump Syndrome: It's the Economics, Stupid* (2016):

[17] Will Dahlgreen, *British Press 'Most Right-Wing' in Europe* (YouGov):

[18] Ian Traynor, 'Europe Set for Bruising Battle over Sharing Refugee Burden' (*The Guardian*, 2015) <https://www.theguardian.com/world/2015/sep/04/eastern-european-leaders-reject-concerted-policy-on-sharing-refugee-burden> accessed 25/11/2016

[19] Ruth Bender and Mohammad Nour Alakraa, 'In Germany, Refugees Provide Terror Tipoffs, but Investigations Prove Tricky' (*The Wall Street Journal*, 2016) <www.wsj.com/articles/germany-grapples-with-refugee-tips-in-terror-probes-1478079001> accessed 26/11/2016

[20] Unknown, 'Afghanistan 1979-1992' (*GlobalSecurity.org*, Unkown) <www.globalsecurity.org/intell/ops/afghanistan.htm> accessed 26/11/2016 ; Martin Beckford, 'National Archives: Britain Agreed Secret Deal to Back Mujahideen' (*The Telegraph*, 2010) <www.telegraph.co.uk/news/worldnews/asia/afghanistan/8215187/National-Archives-Britain-agreed-secret-deal-to-back-Mujahideen.html> accessed 26/11/2016

[21] Thomas Hegghammer, 'The Rise of Muslim Foreign Fighters: Islam and the Globalization of Jihad' (2011):

[22] Paul Byrne, 'Asylum Seekers Booked into Hotel with Pool, Gym, Spa and Sauna by Government Contractor' (*The Mirror*, 2015) <www.mirror.co.uk/news/uk-news/asylum-seekers-booked-hotel-pool-6241861> accessed 26/11/2016

much of this debate, the system is deliberately conflated by right of centre media commentators to include asylum seekers (those awaiting their claims to refugee protective status being processed) who are housed, occasionally in relatively expensive rented accommodation, on the basis that they are realistically and legally unable to support themselves. A confusion over the causation between the influx of refugees and the relative depravation of an area is not in the in the direction that the narrative would suggest; refugees are almost entirely housed in areas which have had high levels of depravation as these are the areas with the most vacant housing and with the population least likely to object, or the capacity to find those with the authority and willingness to do anything about potential complaints from those areas[23]. This has led to a perception that the refugees are a burden, fracturing a finite level of resources among an increasing level of population – the levels of available resources are a consequence of the choice the state has made to not provide those resources in a bit to create a smaller state together the juxtaposition of a contemporary cultural evolution in the way that the population lives[24].

This negative narrative undermines the prospects of effective integration and the possible gains for society: refugees who have been well integrated and treated fairly are generally the greatest ambassadors of a country, having reaped the benefits of the state they go on to espouse the virtues of that state[25]. Refugees are more mobile, generally having no preference to live one area over another, this means that in a country with little in the way of natural resources to exploit, the refugee incumbents can be placed in areas which have suffered as a result of large systemic changes[26], such as the former mining towns of the United Kingdom, in order to support an economic revitalisation – the internal economy of the western democracies is

---

[23] Christopher Hope, 'Eight in 10 Uk Councils - Including Many in Affluent Areas - Fail to Accept a Single Vulnerable Syrian Refugee' (*The Telegraph*, 2016) <www.telegraph.co.uk/news/2016/08/02/eight-in-10-uk-councils---including-many-in-affluent-areas---fai/> accessed 26/11/2016

[24] Michael Yong, 'How Bad Is the Housing Crisis in Bristol? Nearly 10,000 People Waiting for Just 41 Council Homes' (*Bristol Post*, 2016) <www.bristolpost.co.uk/nearly-10-000-people-waiting-just-41-council/story-29298961-detail/story.html> accessed 26/11/2016 ; Unknown, 'Do Refugees Take Away Social Housing Opportunities from Locals?' (*Debating Europe*, 2016) <www.debatingeurope.eu/2016/10/06/refugees-take-away-social-housing-opportunities-locals/#.WDn-oPmLS9I> accessed 26/11/2016

[25] Wikipedia Contributors, 'List of Refugees' (*Wikipedia, The Free Encyclopedia.*, 2016) <https://en.wikipedia.org/w/index.php?title=List_of_refugees&oldid=742884704> accessed 26/11/2016

[26] Claire Jones, 'Refugees May Ease Germany's Problem of a Shrinking Workforce' (*The FT*, 2015) <https://www.ft.com/content/bfd6adfe-47e8-11e5-af2f-4d6e0e5eda22> accessed 26/11/2016

becoming more reliant on people working just to buy items from other people working to buy items, and the real economy has remained relatively static in comparison to other economic activity, such as the financial markets[27]. These refugees are also the ones who have felt that they would have a chance to make a life for themselves in the countries that they have travelled to, so they generally have the personal resources to be able to deal with having little or no help in starting out, they are naturally entrepreneurial, and some cases well educated[28].

The negative narrative also underplays, or completely ignores the encroaching failure that the westernised democracies have been generating for some time; with a low birth rate and an increased ability to cure diseases which would have once killed many at an earlier age, the average age of the population is steadily increasing, this will eventually led to the situation where the level of the population who require care support and are entitled to the pensions that they have contributed to, becomes unsustainable[29]. This narrative might be somewhat more persuasive if the possibility of those have come to the refugee protecting countries can return to the countries where they have left, but this can only be done if the conditions for return are objectively acceptable.

For the return of migrants to be facilitated, the country of origin must be helped to develop an environment which the refugees find attractive, this can only be done in countries which have suffered conflict if they have accepted the rule of law, both internationally and of their own making, and have encouraged a way to respect the property rights of those who have left. It is particularly important for post-conflict countries to have an effective 'truth and reconciliation' process, so that old grudges do not fester and become the fuel for further conflict; although it must be accepted that some conduct will never be punished it is important to air all the grievances and punish the severest of events when appropriate[30]. It is also important that those who have had a legitimate claim to property have recourse for its return, compensation, or at least an effective method of attempting this, so that they can create a home and a means of support[31].

---

[27] Ed Conway, *Just How Imbalanced Is the Uk Economy?* (2014):

[28] Mehul Srivastava, 'Syrian Refugee Entrepreneurs Boost Turkey's Economy' (*The FT*, 2016) <https://www.ft.com/content/93e3d794-1826-11e6-b197-a4af20d5575e> accessed 26/11/2016 ; Arshin Adib-Moghaddam, 'World Insight: Syria Is in Europe' (*The Times Higher Education*, 2016) <https://www.timeshighereducation.com/blog/world-insight-syria-europe> accessed 26/11/2016

[29] Jones, 'Refugees May Ease Germany's Problem of a Shrinking Workforce'

[30] Alfred Allan and Marietjie M Allan, 'The South African Truth and Reconciliation Commission as a Therapeutic Tool' (2000) 18(4) Behavioral sciences & the law 459:

[31] Charles Philpott, 'Though the Dog Is Dead, the Pig Must Be Killed: Finishing

What then for the refugees who choose to remain in the country of refuge; they may do so because of having a family, the children may well have a claim to different citizenships because of their parentage, or at least have a cultural affinity to that nationality rather than the one they have escaped from[32]. Failing to acknowledge that we live in an increasingly small world, where the differences between us is shrinking only allows those who feel like outsiders to the countries in which they live and are outsiders to the country in which their parents have come from, to feel a disconnect from the world they live in[33]. They have a feeling of disaffection from the lack of belonging, and this has historically been very corrosive to both individuals and society, allowing a foothold for the radicalisation of individuals, who like much of society, feel like they have been left behind after being implicitly promised a bright future in their parent's new country[34].

In conclusion, the issue of refugees is one which is instructive of much of our wider society and how we are governed; the parliamentarian Tony Benn is attributed as having said "The way a government treats refugees is very instructive because it shows you how they would treat the rest of us if they thought they could get away with it.", this statement falls short in that it is too narrowly defined; how we treat refugees shows us how we would treat each other, were we to befall a situation where we would require the help of others. But much more than this, it is instructive of how short-sighted we can be; with refugees who have been 'warehoused' in a refugee camp for more than a generation[35], lost to the world but a burden on it at the same time, we are storing up problems for the future, hoping that we can defer the issue indefinitely until it sorts itself out[36]. On the contrary, the issue of refugees is not one which can be solved by the construction of barriers, physically or

---

with Property Restitution to Bosnia-Herzegovina's Idps and Refugees' (2005) 18(1) Journal of Refugee Studies 1:

[32] Madawi Al-Rasheed, 'The Myth of Return: Iraqi Arab and Assyrian Refugees in London' (1994) 7(2-3) ibid| Cited Pages 199:

[33] Will Jennings and others, 'Political Disaffection Is Rising, and Driving Ukip Support' (*YouGov*, 2014) <https://yougov.co.uk/news/2014/10/29/political-disaffection-not-new-it-rising-and-drivi/> accessed 27/11/2016

[34] Alejandro Portes and Alejandro Rivas, 'The Adaptation of Migrant Children' (2011) 21(1) The future of children 219:

[35] Wikipedia Contributors, 'Dadaab' (*Wikipedia, The Free Encyclopedia*, 2016) <https://en.wikipedia.org/w/index.php?title=Dadaab&oldid=748493142> accessed 27/11/2016 ; Murithi Mutiga and Emma Graham-Harrison, 'Kenya Says It Will Shut World's Biggest Refugee Camp at Dadaab' (*Guardian*, 2016) <https://www.theguardian.com/world/2016/may/11/kenya-close-worlds-biggest-refugee-camp-dadaab> accessed 03/09/2016

[36] Nick Bryant, 'Un Focuses on Refugees - Will It Be Enough?' (*BBC*, 2016) <www.bbc.co.uk/news/world-us-canada-37389648> accessed 27/11/2016

metaphorically; unless we work with refugees as a welcomed resource, rather than an unnecessary burden, we will continue to witness a creep in the problems caused by not dealing with the issues.

With this book the contributors hope to highlight a few of the challenges regarding refugees and in some cases, how these challenges might be met.

## References

The 1951 Convention Relating to the Status of Refugees and the 1967 Protocol

Mss V Belgium & Greece (ECtHR)

Abramsky S, 'If Sweden and Denmark Are So Progressive, Why Did They Close Their Doors to Refugees?' (The Nation, 2016) <https://www.thenation.com/article/if-sweden-and-denmark-are-so-progressive-why-did-they-close-their-doors-to-refugees/> accessed 25/11/2016

Adib-Moghaddam A, 'World Insight: Syria Is in Europe' (The Times Higher Education, 2016) <https://www.timeshighereducation.com/blog/world-insight-syria-europe> accessed 26/11/2016

Al-Rasheed M, 'The Myth of Return: Iraqi Arab and Assyrian Refugees in London' (1994) 7(2-3) Journal of Refugee Studies 199

Allan A and Allan MM, 'The South African Truth and Reconciliation Commission as a Therapeutic Tool' (2000) 18(4) Behavioral sciences & the law 459

Beckford M, 'National Archives: Britain Agreed Secret Deal to Back Mujahideen' (The Telegraph, 2010) <www.telegraph.co.uk/news/worldnews/asia/afghanistan/8215187/National-Archives-Britain-agreed-secret-deal-to-back-Mujahideen.html> accessed 26/11/2016

BENDER R and ALAKRAA MN, 'In Germany, Refugees Provide Terror Tipoffs, but Investigations Prove Tricky' (The Wall Street Journal, 2016) <www.wsj.com/articles/germany-grapples-with-refugee-tips-in-terror-probes-1478079001> accessed 26/11/2016

Bryant N, 'Un Focuses on Refugees - Will It Be Enough?' (BBC, 2016) <www.bbc.co.uk/news/world-us-canada-37389648> accessed 27/11/2016

BYRNE P, 'Asylum Seekers Booked into Hotel with Pool, Gym, Spa and Sauna by Government Contractor' (The Mirror, 2015) <www.mirror.co.uk/news/uk-news/asylum-seekers-booked-hotel-pool-6241861> accessed 26/11/2016

Chater J, 'What Are the Consequences of Brexit for the Refugee Crisis?' (The New Statesman, 2016) <www.newstatesman.com/politics/uk/2016/06/what-are-consequences-brexit-refugee-crisis> accessed 25/11/2016

contributors W, 'Dadaab' (Wikipedia, The Free Encyclopedia, 2016) <https://en.wikipedia.org/w/index.php?title=Dadaab&oldid=748493142> accessed 27/11/2016

contributors W, 'List of Refugees' (Wikipedia, The Free Encyclopedia., 2016) <https://en.wikipedia.org/w/index.php?title=List_of_refugees&oldid=742884704> accessed 26/11/2016

Conway E, Just How Imbalanced Is the Uk Economy? (2014)

Dahlgreen W, British Press 'Most Right-Wing' in Europe (YouGov)

Dearden L, 'How Economic Migrants Become Refugees as They Seek a New Life' (2016) <www.independent.co.uk/news/world/europe/refugees-economic-migrants-europe-crisis-difference-middle-east-africa-libya-mediterranean-sea-a7432516.html> accessed 25/11/2016

Dearden L, 'Hungary Planning 'Massive' New Border Fence to Keep out Refugees as Pm Vows to 'Hold Them Back by Force'' (The Independent, 2016) <www.independent.co.uk/news/world/europe/hungary-massive-new-border-fence-to-keep-out-refugees-prime-minister-orban-turkey-eu-hold-them-back-a7212696.html> accessed 25/11/2016

Dearden L, 'Majority of Refugees Arriving in Europe Never Wanted to Come to Continent' (The Independent, 2016) <www.independent.co.uk/news/world/europe/refugees-europe-never-wanted-to-come-libya-mediterranean-deaths-economic-migrants-torture-abuse-a7432066.html> accessed 25/11/2016

Editorial, 'Dentists Condemn Call for Child Migrants' Teeth to Be Tested' (BBC, 2016) <www.bbc.co.uk/news/uk-37700074> accessed 19/10/2016

Editorial, 'Eu Policy Pushes Refugees to Illegal Travel Routes' (The New Arab, 2015) <https://www.alaraby.co.uk/english/politics/2015/6/22/eu-policy-pushes-refugees-to-illegal-travel-routes> accessed 25/11/2016

Editorial, 'Migrant Crisis: What Is the Uk Doing to Help?' (BBC, 2016) <http://www.bbc.co.uk/news/uk-34139960> accessed 25/11/2016

Gambino L and Kingsley P, 'Refugees in Us Nervously Await Trump Presidency after Campaign Rhetoric' (The Guardian, 2016) <https://www.theguardian.com/us-news/2016/nov/24/refugees-in-us-trump-administration-syria> accessed 25/11/2016

Hall A and Lichfield J, 'Germany Opens Its Gates: Berlin Says All Syrian Asylum-Seekers Are Welcome to Remain, as Britain Is Urged to Make a 'Similar Statement'' (The Independent, 2015) <www.independent.co.uk/news/world/europe/germany-opens-its-gates-berlin-says-all-syrian-asylum-seekers-are-welcome-to-remain-as-britain-is-10470062.html> accessed 25/11/2016

HARRIS D and JESKO J, 'Anti-Immigrant Protests Grow as Thousands of Refugees Flood Europe' (ABC News, 2015) <http://abcnews.go.com/International/anti-immigrant-protests-grow-thousands-refugees-flood-europe/story?id=35888428> accessed 25/11/2016

Hegghammer T, 'The Rise of Muslim Foreign Fighters: Islam and the Globalization of Jihad' (2011)

Hope C, 'Eight in 10 Uk Councils - Including Many in Affluent Areas - Fail to Accept a Single Vulnerable Syrian Refugee' (The Telegraph, 2016) <www.telegraph.co.uk/news/2016/08/02/eight-in-10-uk-councils---including-many-in-affluent-areas---fai/> accessed 26/11/2016

Jacobs M and Mazzucato M, The Brexit-Trump Syndrome: It's the Economics, Stupid (2016)

Jennings W and others, 'Political Disaffection Is Rising, and Driving Ukip Support' (YouGov, 2014) <https://yougov.co.uk/news/2014/10/29/political-disaffection-not-new-it-rising-and-drivi/> accessed 27/11/2016

JONES A, 'I've Seen First Hand How Easily Our Asylum System Can Be Abused – and There's No Real Way to Stop It' (The Telegraph, 2016) <www.telegraph.co.uk/news/2016/10/30/ive-seen-first-hand-how-easily-our-asylum-system-can-be-abused/> accessed 25/11/2016

Jones C, 'Refugees May Ease Germany's Problem of a Shrinking Workforce' (The FT, 2015) <https://www.ft.com/content/bfd6adfe-47e8-11e5-af2f-4d6e0e5eda22> accessed 26/11/2016

Kingsley P, 'Refugees Enter Croatia from Serbia after Hungary Blocks Border' (The Guardian, 2015) <https://www.theguardian.com/world/2015/sep/16/refugees-enter-croatia-from-serbia-after-hungary-blocks-border> accessed 25/11/2016

Mayblin L, Asylum Seekers in Britain: Putting the Economic 'Pull Factor' in Context (LSE 2016)

Mughan A and Paxton P, 'Anti-Immigrant Sentiment, Policy Preferences and Populist Party Voting in Australia' (2006) 36(British Journal of Political Science 341

Mutiga M and Graham-Harrison E, 'Kenya Says It Will Shut World's Biggest Refugee Camp at Dadaab' (Guardian, 2016) <https://www.theguardian.com/world/2016/may/11/kenya-close-worlds-biggest-refugee-camp-dadaab> accessed 03/09/2016

Palazzo C, 'Norway Offers to Pay Asylum Seekers £1000 Bonus to Leave the Country' (The Telegraph, 2016) <www.telegraph.co.uk/news/2016/04/26/norway-to-pay-asylum-seekers-extra-money-to-leave/> accessed 25/11/2016

Philpott C, 'Though the Dog Is Dead, the Pig Must Be Killed: Finishing with Property Restitution to Bosnia-Herzegovina's Idps and Refugees' (2005) 18(1) Journal of Refugee Studies 1

Portes A and Rivas A, 'The Adaptation of Migrant Children' (2011) 21(1) The future of children 219

Schloenhardt A, 'To Deter, Detain and Deny : Protection of Onshore Asylum Seekers in Australia' (2002) 14(2-3) International journal of refugee law International journal of refugee law 302

SMALE A, 'Flooded with Migrants, Germany Struggles to Integrate Them' (The New York Times, 2016) <www.nytimes.com/2016/04/28/world/europe/germany-migrants-struggles-to-integrate.html?_r=0> accessed 25/11/2016

Srivastava M, 'Syrian Refugee Entrepreneurs Boost Turkey's Economy' (The FT, 2016) <https://www.ft.com/content/93e3d794-1826-11e6-b197-a4af20d5575e> accessed 26/11/2016

Traynor I, 'Europe Set for Bruising Battle over Sharing Refugee Burden' (The Guardian, 2015) <https://www.theguardian.com/world/2015/sep/04/eastern-european-leaders-reject-concerted-policy-on-sharing-refugee-burden> accessed 25/11/2016

Traynor I, 'Italy Threatens to Give Schengen Visas to Migrants as Eu Ministers Meet' (The Guardian, 2015) <https://www.theguardian.com/world/2015/jun/15/italy-threatens-to-give-schengen-visas-to-migrants-as-eu-dispute-deepens> accessed 25/11/2016

Unknown, 'Afghanistan 1979-1992' (GlobalSecurity.org, Unkown) <www.globalsecurity.org/intell/ops/afghanistan.htm> accessed 26/11/2016

Unknown, 'Do Refugees Take Away Social Housing Opportunities from Locals?' (Debating Europe, 2016) <www.debatingeurope.eu/2016/10/06/refugees-take-away-social-housing-opportunities-locals/#.WDn-oPmLS9I> accessed 26/11/2016

Wright O, 'Eu Referendum: Nigel Farage's Anti-Migrant Poster Like 1930s Fascist Propaganda, Says George Osborne' (The Independent, 2016) <www.independent.co.uk/news/uk/politics/eu-referendum-poster-nigel-farage-polls-michael-gove-a7089946.html> accessed 25/11/2016

Yong M, 'How Bad Is the Housing Crisis in Bristol? Nearly 10,000 People Waiting for Just 41 Council Homes' (Bristol Post, 2016) <www.bristolpost.co.uk/nearly-10-000-people-waiting-just-41-council/story-29298961-detail/story.html> accessed 26/11/2016

# Introduction

## Robert W. Reed

The 20th and 21st centuries have seen the world involved in wars which have been completely unlike those that have gone before the, wars which have encompassed entire continents, or have had no distinct 'field of battle'[37]. These wars led to an interconnectedness of states which helped defeat aggressors and bring about a forum in which states could air their grievances as equals, rather than relying on the gun and bomb to solve these challenges, as had gone before: Thus, came about; firstly, the League of Nations, then the United Nations; both imperfect, but a product of pragmatism.

This interconnectedness gave rise to a new term 'Globalisation' a paradigm where the state you are a citizen of was not the only provider of services to you, nor was it the only protection; the atrocities of the second world war put pay to the paradigm that the state could treat its citizens with impunity within its own borders. Globalisation also facilitated the idea that citizens of a state were also fluid in their membership to that state, they no longer remained in their state as a matter of course; they migrated in order to seek the betterment of themselves, while others did so in order to seek protection of the state which could do so[38].

The lines between who would, should, and could, seek protection soon became blurred due to the perceptions of the populations within the protecting state, the ease with which one could travel the planet, and the extent to which state borders have become increasingly irrelevant to the ordinary person on the 'Clapham Omnibus'[39].

In the globalised system, the state no longer has the monopoly on the use of force, where the use of warfare was once confined between states, it has now reached the point where non-state actors and states engage in warfare on relatively

---

[37] Philip Bobbitt, *The Shield of Achilles: War, Peace, and the Course of History* (Anchor 2007)

[38] Philip Bobbitt, *Terror and Consent: The Wars of the Twenty-First Century* (Anchor 2009)

[39] Liza Schuster, 'Turning Refugees into 'Illegal Migrants': Afghan Asylum Seekers in Europe' (2011) 34 Ethnic and Racial studies 1392:

equal terms, thanks to the use of asymmetric warfare, and the insurgents use of the cover of the ordinary population as cover for their nefarious activities[40]. This act of blending into the crowd also becomes a source of paranoia and propaganda to the protective state by the insurgent group; as it need only introduce the idea of the inclusion of terrorists among refugees for the level of paranoia to become a weapon of war in of itself, the mantra 'better to err on the side of caution' becomes the domain of the far-right rhetoricians, which both becomes a clumsy 'truism' and a self-fulfilling prophecy, when established populations in the protector state become radicalised thanks to the treatment meted out from well-meaning adherents of the truism[41].

The stereotype that refugees harbour terrorists or are economic migrants has become so resonant with the public, that the state has become quick to change the definitions of their sovereign territory, using one definition of a border in one situation while using a definition specifically in regard to claims of refugee status in another[42].

Globalisation also brought other problems to bear; long held views were countered so effectively, but so maladroitly that while it became socially unacceptable to express views which were xenophobic, or otherwise discriminatory, it also became a rhetorical bludgeon with which to stifle debate, this in turn was countered with cries of those who recognised this fact, that the imposition of xenophobia was only raised, not because the acts were xenophobic, but that it was merely a cynical ploy to end a debate which the accuser was otherwise losing the moral high ground of; the consequence of this was a paralysis of critical debate over matters which were deemed to be 'multiculturalism'[43].

This paralysis manifested itself in two ways: Firstly, negative aspects of culture were placed out of bounds by mainstream debate for fear of being seen being xenophobic, or bigoted, this vacuum was inhabited by the right and the nuanced sections of the far-right, but particularly by the hard-right (or radical right) political parties; and by a process of frame extension these groups garnered support from those who had concerns about 'multiculturalism' but had erstwhile been unable to

---

[40] Thomas Pm Barnett, *Great Powers: America and the World after Bush* (Penguin 2009)

[41] Maggie Ibrahim, 'The Securitization of Migration: A Racial Discourse1' (2005) 43 International migration 163:

[42] Jennifer Hyndman and Alison Mountz, 'Another Brick in the Wall? Neo-Refoulement and the Externalization of Asylum by Australia and Europe1' (2008) 43 Government and Opposition 249:

[43] Les Back and others, 'New Labour's White Heart: Politics, Multiculturalism and the Return of Assimilation' (2002) 73 The Political Quarterly 445:

support any groups previously, due to the views of those groups on race, religion and other ideals on equality[44].

Secondly, the established populations came to perceive the state as giving new migrants in general more support than the established population, a point which was capitalised upon by the media, further breeding discontent[45].

The paralysis allowed, the British government in particular, to acquiesce known extremists and radicals to seek asylum in the UK on the basis that it was an unwritten covenant, if the UK gave refugee protection to those persons, they in return would not perpetrate acts of terror towards the UK[46].

This covenant largely worked until the mid-1990's when the west was seen as acquiescing to the genocide and 'ethnic cleansing' of the mainly Muslim *Bosniaks (and Croats)*, although the western alliance had gone to great lengths, despite major legal flaws, to protect the Muslim population from the Bosnian Serb army[47].

Many radicalised youths travelled to the Balkans in order to support their fellow Muslims, many of which had been battle hardened by over a decade of warfare against the Soviet Army in Afghanistan as Mujahideen fighters who had formerly been supported by the US CIA in that fight[48].

The brutal conflict left a lasting effect, a scar on the international community of states that had been involved in the peacekeeping operation, and as a result many nations vowed to avoid operations under the guise of the UN. The resulting refugees from the conflict dispersed themselves throughout Europe and the west and awaited the day that they could return to the home that they had been forced to leave[49]. Hodzic's paper deals with the manner in which Bosnia and Herzegovina has

---

[44] Oliver Gruber and Tim Bale, 'And It's Good Night Vienna. How (Not) to Deal with the Populist Radical Right: The Conservatives, Ukip and Some Lessons from the Heartland' (2014) 9 British Politics 237:

[45] Martin Beckford, '£886million... That Is the Eye-Watering Sum You Pay in Benefits to out-of-Work Eu Migrants in Just One Year' *The Daily Mail* (28 February 2016) <http://www.dailymail.co.uk/news/article-3467563/886million-eye-watering-sum-pay-benefits-work-EU-migrants-just-one-year.html>

[46] Lewis Herrington, 'Incubating Extremist Terrorism: The Uk Islamic Fundamentalist Movement 1989-2014', University of Warwick 2015)

[47] Ibid

[48] Jason Burke, 'Frankenstein the Cia Created: Mujahideen Trained and Funded by the Us Are among Its Deadliest Foes' (1999) 1 The Guardian 17:

[49] Erin D Mooney, 'Presence, Ergo Protection? Unprofor, Unhcr and the Icrc in Croatia and Bosnia and Herzegovina' (1995) 7 International journal of refugee law 407:

managed to deal with one common barrier to the return of refugees to their country of origin, the issue of land rights in returnees.

The end of the conflict led to yet further challenges, the citizens that had gone to fight in support of the Muslims in the Balkans were now also battle hardened, but radicalised with the teachings of a form of political Islam which espoused violence and a caliphate to the problem of nationalist wars, and xenophobic hate towards the 'west' for a failure to prevent much of the violence that occurred; additionally, many that had gone to fight, had seen their battle against the – mainly Christian - Serbians and Croatians in a positive light[50].

Some of the more militant elements of the Mujahideen were already disaffected by the west, who during the Gulf war, almost a decade before, had been stationed in the holy land of Saudi Arabia, and saw this as a slight against them, particularly as they had offered to protect the region without the help of the west; this as yet, had not become a unifying element though. However, a particular number of Mujahideen had become a group in their own right around two years before the Gulf war, and as such were in the position to provide expertise behind a campaign against those who had incurred their wrath for their trespasses upon their holy land, they were the, now infamous group, Al Qaeda (AQ) and their leader, Osama Bin Laden [51].

The AQ brand – as there have been numerous spinoffs – has found an ability to resist destruction by states by operating within states whose government's tolerated, or were just powerless to do anything about them operating within their borders, such as Yemen[52] and Afghanistan[53], these states found themselves a target of a military campaign by the US following the attacks of 9/11[54] on the basis of the US President, George W Bush's statement 'You're either with us, or you're against us'[55].

---

[50] Jeni Mitchell, 'The Contradictory Effects of Ideology on Jihadist War-Fighting: The Bosnia Precedent' (2008) 31 Studies in Conflict & Terrorism 808: ; Tony Barber, 'The Bosnia Crisis: Serbs, Croats and Muslims: Who Hates Who and Why: Tony Barber in Zagreb Traces the Ancient Roots of a Culture Clash That Has Shattered What Was Yugoslavia into Warring Pieces' *The Independent* (8 August 1992) <http://www.independent.co.uk/news/world/the-bosnia-crisis-serbs-croats-and-muslims-who-hates-who-and-why-tony-barber-in-zagreb-traces-the-1539305.html>

[51] Andrew Wander, 'A History of Terror: Al-Qaeda 1988-2008' (*The Observer*, 2008) <https://www.theguardian.com/world/2008/jul/13/history.alqaida> accessed 08/08/2016

[52] April Longley Alley, 'Yemen's Multiple Crises' (2010) 21 Journal of Democracy 72:

[53] Editorial, 'Al-Qaeda's Origins and Links' (*BBC.co.uk*, 2004) <http://news.bbc.co.uk/1/hi/world/middle_east/1670089.stm> accessed 03/09/2016

[54] Unknown, '911memorial.Org' 2016) <http://www.911memorial.org/> accessed

Together with an already ongoing campaign in Iraq, to find Weapons of Mass Destruction, the world became increasing more unstable; where once there had been absolute rule by authoritarian and autocratic leaders in much of the region, they were swapped for more democratic leaders, or democratic structures were encouraged through support for the revolutionary forces, which had come out of the 'Arab Spring', by states such as the US, and UK[56].

The instability in the MENA region and Afghanistan spilled over into the surrounding regions, with an eventual conflict happening in Syria following a harsh drought, and the NATO ally, Turkey having more troubles of its own, through its Kurdish separatist movement[57]. As a result, the region became an exporter of refugees, with more than 25% of Syria's population leaving the country to seek refuge, mainly in the surrounding states[58].

Returning to a concurrent period to the conflict occurring in the Balkans, many African states, whose authoritarian regimes had been for decades propped up by either the Soviet Union, or the United States in a proxy war, began to lose their support, both materiel and economic as the Soviet Union collapsed and the US began to see no further utility in supporting these regimes in the absence of any need to support the regimes[59]. Without support, the authoritarian regimes fell to the ideologically motivated groups of jihadists and those who were merely using the opportunity to make money or obtain power[60]; as a result, large numbers of people,

---

03/09/2016

[55] Editorial, ''You Are Either with Us or against Us'' (*CNN.com*, 2001) <http://edition.cnn.com/2001/US/11/06/gen.attack.on.terror/> accessed 03/09/2016

[56] Garry Blight, Sheila Pulham and Paul Torpey, 'Arab Spring: An Interactive Timeline of Middle East Protests' (*Guardian*, 2012) <http://www.theguardian.com/world/interactive/2011/mar/22/middle-east-protest-interactive-timeline> accessed 03/09/2016

[57] Bbc Monitoring, 'Turkey V Syria's Kurds V Islamic State' (*BBC.co.uk*, 2016) <http://www.bbc.co.uk/news/world-middle-east-33690060> accessed 03/09/2016

[58] Unhcr, 'Syria Regional Refugee Response' (*UNHCR*, 2016) <http://data.unhcr.org/syrianrefugees/regional.php> accessed 03/09/2016 ; Unknown, 'Syria Population' (*Countrymeters*, 2016) <http://countrymeters.info/en/Syria> accessed 03/09/2016

[59] Wikipedia Contributors, 'List of Proxy Wars' (*Wikipedia, The Free Encyclopedia.*, 2016) <https://en.wikipedia.org/w/index.php?title=List_of_proxy_wars&oldid=737503832> accessed 03/09/2016 ; Mumbi Z. Ngugi, 'Why Kenya Is on the Frontline of New Proxy Wars in Africa' (*Business Daily*, 2015) <http://www.businessdailyafrica.com/Opinion-and-Analysis/Kenya-frontline-of-new-proxy-wars-in-Africa/539548-2678622-853svf/index.html> accessed 03/09/2016

[60] Ngugi, 'Why Kenya Is on the Frontline of New Proxy Wars in Africa'

who had little or nothing to do with the internal conflicts, were caught in the crossfire.

Unable to rely on the protection of their state or unwilling to do so for fear of being a target of the state's retribution, large numbers of populations moved to the more stable and affluent neighbouring states, such as Kenya. These States became to perceive the new incumbents as a tolerated squatter in the country, not integrating them, but as a developed country with a reputation to uphold, unable to pass them on to other places; the incumbent refugee population were warehoused in large camps while the state tried to mitigate the numbers joining the diaspora group by interpreting the state's jurisdiction, and therefore its responsibility in a flexible and subjective manner; Ngugi's paper deals with the new territorial regime of creating fluidly defined borders, where the territorial limits of a state's jurisdiction are subjectively defined by the purpose and person entering that territory.

After several decades of hosting the refugees, and a number of jihadist attacks, Kenya has taken the decision to close the world's largest refugee camp, Dabaab[61]. This will provide further impetus for the refugees to seek refuge in more stable countries, even as far afield as Europe, where the far-right narrative of the refugee migrants as terrorists has gained some traction following attacks by jihadists who have been citizens of European states with foreign familial origins[62]. This narrative is further exasperated by erroneous understandings of the concept of human rights by the public in general, and the failures of the state, who find a convenient scapegoat in human rights legislation and international law obligations towards refugees, Reed's paper seeks to shed light on the issue and highlight to tools that are available to the state in order to protect the population from not only terrorist suspects, but war criminals and those who may have committed serious crimes and have feigned persecution in order to avoid prosecution.

Underpinning this tension of obligation, legal constraint, and the motivations of the state to look after itself, and not those from elsewhere, Prof Sait has helpfully outlined two chapters for this framework analysis, one on the legal, and the remainder on the human rights aspect of refugee-dom.

---

[61] Murithi Mutiga and Emma Graham-Harrison, 'Kenya Says It Will Shut World's Biggest Refugee Camp at Dadaab' (*Guardian*, 2016) <https://www.theguardian.com/world/2016/may/11/kenya-close-worlds-biggest-refugee-camp-dadaab> accessed 03/09/2016

[62] Editorial, 'Paris Attacks' (*BBC.co.uk*, 2016) <http://www.bbc.co.uk/news/world-europe-30717580> accessed 03/09/2016

# References

Alley AL, 'Yemen's Multiple Crises' (2010) 21 Journal of Democracy 72

Back L and others, 'New Labour's White Heart: Politics, Multiculturalism and the Return of Assimilation' (2002) 73 The Political Quarterly 445

Barber T, 'The Bosnia Crisis: Serbs, Croats and Muslims: Who Hates Who and Why: Tony Barber in Zagreb Traces the Ancient Roots of a Culture Clash That Has Shattered What Was Yugoslavia into Warring Pieces' The Independent (8 August 1992) <http://www.independent.co.uk/news/world/the-bosnia-crisis-serbs-croats-and-muslims-who-hates-who-and-why-tony-barber-in-zagreb-traces-the-1539305.html>

Barnett TP, Great Powers: America and the World after Bush (Penguin 2009)

BECKFORD M, '£886million... That Is the Eye-Watering Sum You Pay in Benefits to out-of-Work Eu Migrants in Just One Year' The Daily Mail (28 February 2016) <http://www.dailymail.co.uk/news/article-3467563/886million-eye-watering-sum-pay-benefits-work-EU-migrants-just-one-year.html>

Blight G, Pulham S and Torpey P, 'Arab Spring: An Interactive Timeline of Middle East Protests' (Guardian, 2012) <http://www.theguardian.com/world/interactive/2011/mar/22/middle-east-protest-interactive-timeline> accessed 03/09/2016

Bobbitt P, The Shield of Achilles: War, Peace, and the Course of History (Anchor 2007)

Bobbitt P, Terror and Consent: The Wars of the Twenty-First Century (Anchor 2009)

Burke J, 'Frankenstein the Cia Created: Mujahideen Trained and Funded by the Us Are among Its Deadliest Foes' (1999) 1 The Guardian 17

contributors W, 'List of Proxy Wars' (Wikipedia, The Free Encyclopedia., 2016) <https://en.wikipedia.org/w/index.php?title=List_of_proxy_wars&oldid=737503832> accessed 03/09/2016

Editorial, 'Al-Qaeda's Origins and Links' (BBC.co.uk, 2004) <http://news.bbc.co.uk/1/hi/world/middle_east/1670089.stm> accessed 03/09/2016

Editorial, 'Paris Attacks' (BBC.co.uk, 2016) <http://www.bbc.co.uk/news/world-europe-30717580> accessed 03/09/2016

Editorial, ''You Are Either with Us or against Us'' (CNN.com, 2001) <http://edition.cnn.com/2001/US/11/06/gen.attack.on.terror/> accessed 03/09/2016

Gruber O and Bale T, 'And It's Good Night Vienna. How (Not) to Deal with the Populist Radical Right: The Conservatives, Ukip and Some Lessons from the Heartland' (2014) 9 British Politics 237

Herrington L, 'Incubating Extremist Terrorism: The Uk Islamic Fundamentalist Movement 1989-2014' (University of Warwick 2015)

Hyndman J and Mountz A, 'Another Brick in the Wall? Neo-Refoulement and the Externalization of Asylum by Australia and Europe1' (2008) 43 Government and Opposition 249

Ibrahim M, 'The Securitization of Migration: A Racial Discourse1' (2005) 43 International migration 163

Mitchell J, 'The Contradictory Effects of Ideology on Jihadist War-Fighting: The Bosnia Precedent' (2008) 31 Studies in Conflict & Terrorism 808

Monitoring B, 'Turkey V Syria's Kurds V Islamic State' (BBC.co.uk, 2016) <http://www.bbc.co.uk/news/world-middle-east-33690060> accessed 03/09/2016

Mooney ED, 'Presence, Ergo Protection? Unprofor, Unhcr and the Icrc in Croatia and Bosnia and Herzegovina' (1995) 7 International journal of refugee law 407

Mutiga M and Graham-Harrison E, 'Kenya Says It Will Shut World's Biggest Refugee Camp at Dadaab' (Guardian, 2016) <https://www.theguardian.com/world/2016/may/11/kenya-close-worlds-biggest-refugee-camp-dadaab> accessed 03/09/2016

NGUGI MZ, 'Why Kenya Is on the Frontline of New Proxy Wars in Africa' (Business Daily, 2015) <http://www.businessdailyafrica.com/Opinion-and-Analysis/Kenya-frontline-of-new-proxy-wars-in-Africa/539548-2678622-853svf/index.html> accessed 03/09/2016

Schuster L, 'Turning Refugees into 'Illegal Migrants': Afghan Asylum Seekers in Europe' (2011) 34 Ethnic and Racial studies 1392

UNHCR, 'Syria Regional Refugee Response' (UNHCR, 2016) <http://data.unhcr.org/syrianrefugees/regional.php> accessed 03/09/2016

Unknown, '911memorial.Org' (2016) <http://www.911memorial.org/> accessed 03/09/2016

Unknown, 'Syria Population' (Countrymeters, 2016) <http://countrymeters.info/en/Syria> accessed 03/09/2016

Wander A, 'A History of Terror: Al-Qaeda 1988-2008' (The Observer, 2008) <https://www.theguardian.com/world/2008/jul/13/history.alqaida> accessed 08/08/2016

# From Refugee Rights Principles To Rights Based Approaches

## M Siraj Sait

> *Human rights approaches to protection of refugees are a significant layer in global negotiations and strategies. The consistency of human rights outputs, the durability of procedures and their ability to provide succour to different categories of displaced persons is still uncertain. For several decades following the 1951 Convention on the Status of Refugees, the refugee remained merely an object of State adjustments and coordination rather than a central figure exerting direct choices over his or her status or treatment. International refugee legal regime seemed oblivious to the changing nature of the refugee phenomenon, the increase in the number of refugees worldwide, the diversity of refugee experiences and the specific issues relating to refugee women, children and the internally displaced. However, even the most exclusionary refugee frameworks today have to contend with the human rights standards which have achieved consensus among nations at least in theory.*

To speak of refugee rights in 1951 need not have been radical, for the Refugee Convention itself used the terminology of 'rights' over two dozen times. However, the mainstreaming and development of a rights-based approach to construe and implement the Convention had been a tentative and painstaking journey. Though States acknowledged the need for bilateral or multilateral solutions to cross boundary forced migration, policies towards forced migrants were viewed largely as a matter of State discretion with limited international accountability, if it all. As it gained momentum, the recognition of the refugee as a primary stakeholder in the refugee discourse sought to challenge the foundations of a refugee law driven by sovereignty and territorial integrity. This chapter considers how despite law's resistance, the campaign for refugee rights has significantly altered the theoretical assumptions underlying refugee policies and provided the basis for the contemporary debates over the nature and form of international responses to the refugee issue.

The human rights infusion into international refugee regimes has made a perceptible difference with regard to articulation of refugee protection. Certainly, human rights have provided normative depth and sophistication, clarification of expectations and standards relating to refugee rights as well as strategies in seeking formulations of accountability and redress. Yet, the human rights approach to refugee protection clearly has its limits[63]. The potency of human rights argumentation has not been matched with commensurate structural responses leaving open the gap between principles and practice and between rights and remedies. In any case, factors such as globalisation and development, terrorism and civil wars, culture wars and national politics and a host of other factors have rendered refugee rights contested, inconsistent and often unreliable. Refugee rights continue to struggle to attain parity with other sets of human rights where the beneficiaries are citizens or nationals. The automatic location of refugee rights as a sub-sect of the human rights discourse fails to problematize the refugee struggle and its distinctive challenges.

If there is global consensus that refugees have inalienable rights, this is not apparent in the refugee world. The most obvious problem is that human rights appear more effective in some contexts and virtually non-existent in others. Are these rights then contingent and reside in circumstances rather than in people? The refugee discourse continually bemoans the lack of respect, dignity and protection afforded to forced migrants at virtually every stage of their experience. From a human rights perspective, the cause of refugee flight is due to human rights violations and their rights are continually compromised during their quest for protection. The refugee rights dossier is laden with multiple concerns including freedom from persecution, freedom of movement, freedom to seek asylum, access to fair hearing, freedom from detention, right to family reunification, welfare support, education, right to non-discrimination, protection from expulsion and extradition, and the right not to be penalized for 'illegal' entry or stay[64].

Human rights of refugees are actively promoted through over simplification as if the problem lies only in the lack of political will to implement. Yet, the process of identifying, acknowledging and entrenching these rights can be complex. Refugee law using a rights perspective has to contend with the questions of legitimacy and double standards permeating the human rights discourse itself from disputes over

---

[63] Patricia Tuitt, *False Images: Law's Construction of the Refugee* (Pluto Pr 1996)
[64] United Nations High Commissioner for Refugees, *The State of the World's Refugees 2006: Human Displacement in the New Millennium* (2006):

normative content and problems of enforcement[65]. As much as the aggregation of human rights and humanitarian protection standards serve to enhance advocacy, augmenting protection of refugees has turned out to be inherently complex and difficult. While expectations have been high, human rights can only offer complementary protection to the basic needs of refugees who are in the hands of States. It is the interplay between legislators, judges, civil society, academics and others within the sphere of refugee law which determines the durability of refugee rights protection domestically.

The purpose of this chapter is not to systematically identify the applicable refugee norms, to demonstrate the gap between principles and practice, to outline landmark human rights court cases or even to evaluate the strategies adopted by refugee support groups. These themes have been dealt competently elsewhere. This chapter considers three fundamental refugee rights themes. First, is 'human rights' a stable and reliable framework easily deployed for refugee protection? Second, is normative consensus on contentious refugee issues possible, particularly in the post 9/11 world? Third, are refugee rights capable of being enforced in line with refugee needs? This leads to an overview of some current proposals regarding human rights and refugee law reform.

## Exploring Refugee Rights

The Refugee Convention ought to have been a human rights instrument from the beginning. It was drafted as a result of a recommendation by the newly established United Nations Commission on Human Rights and in the context of widespread wartime persecution and displacement. The 1948 Universal Declaration of Human Rights (UDHR) had already declared everyone's right to life, liberty and security of person (Article 3) as well as a right to seek and enjoy asylum (Article 13). Not only were refugees obviously included in the 'human rights for everyone' language[66], they were understood to be a unique category of human rights victims to whom special protection and benefits were due[67]. Drafted around the same period and in a similar context as the UDHR, the beginning (preamble) of the 1951 Refugee Convention is not surprising

---

[65] Anne F Bayefsky, *United Nations Human Rights Treaty System: Universality at the Crossroads* (Martinus Nijhoff Publishers 2001)

[66] Brian Gorlick, 'Human Rights and Refugees: Enhancing Protection through International Human Rights Law' (2000) 69 Nordic Journal of International Law 117; Frances Nicholson and Patrick M Twomey, *Refugee Rights and Realities: Evolving International Concepts and Regimes* (Cambridge University Press Cambridge, UK 1999)

[67] Alice Edwards, 'Human Rights, Refugees, and the Right 'to Enjoy'asylum' (2005) 17 International Journal of Refugee Law 293

Considering that the Charter of the United Nations and the Universal Declaration of Human Rights approved on 10 December 1948 by the General Assembly have affirmed the principle that human beings shall enjoy fundamental rights and freedoms without discrimination......

Some argue that the Refugee Convention itself, including its definition has to be understood through the UDHR[68].

However, that Refugee Convention did not conceive of refugee rights in the same mould of human rights belong to nationals with State protection or within their states of origin. The title 'Convention on the Status of Refugees' itself indicates that the treaty is primarily about legal 'status' as determined by States, not human rights. Thus, the Convention is better known for its laborious endeavour to define refugees rather than empowerment of refugees. In contrast to other human rights conventions, it opens up its substantive section, not by referring to the rights of refugees but rather their obligations towards the host state (Article 2). However, it is followed by principles of non-discrimination (Article 3), non-refoulement (Article 33) and a host of other civil and political rights as well as socio-economic rights. These are significant guarantees for refugees, though the Refugee Convention chooses to provide parity in treatment for refugees with nationals on some rights, not on others. The contrast in both the choice of rights as well as their formulation to the UDHR is striking.

The 1951 Refugee Convention, though widely ratified and used by refugee advocates, has not attained the same status as the six main human rights instruments which followed the UDHR. These six are the 1965 International Convention on the Elimination of All Forms of Racial Discrimination (ICERD), 1966 International Convention on Civil and Political Rights (ICCPR), the 1966 International Covenant on Economic, Social and Cultural Rights (ICESCR), the 1979 Convention on the Elimination of All Forms of Discrimination against Women (CEDAW), 1984 Convention against Torture and Other Cruel, Inhuman or Degrading Treatment or Punishment (CAT) and the 1989 Convention on the Rights of the Child (CRC). The inferiority of the Refugee Convention is underscored by its normative generality and its reluctance to pin direct obligations on States. Critically, it has no direct monitoring and supervisory mechanism (see Chapter VI of the Refugee Convention). Unlike the six main human rights treaties which provide for their own supervisory mechanisms, the implementation of the Refugee Convention is left largely to the States.

---

[68] Michael J Parrish, 'Redefining the Refugee: The Universal Declaration of Human Rights as a Basis for Refugee Protection' (2000) 22 Cardozo L Rev 223

The Refugee Convention, however, was never meant to be a standalone treaty for human rights treaties are inter-related[69]. Article 5 clarifies that "nothing in this Convention shall be deemed to impair any rights and benefits granted by a Contracting State to refugees apart from this Convention". In interpreting the Convention, for example the terms in its definition, recourse to other human rights treaties has been beneficial. Jaquemet[70] talks about how refugee lawyers were compelled to look elsewhere

International refugee lawyers sometimes have a problem of identity. They are used to living in a small cosy house, of which they know each room and cranny and, if any, each hidden place. After all, the 1951 Refugee Convention and its 1967 Protocol, taken together, contain less than 60 articles....The problem is that this tiny house cannot accommodate refugee protection in its entirety. Whereas the codification process has been put on hold, the refugee problem has inexorably grown in scope, magnitude and complexity. The logical — and rather pragmatic — response has been non-treaty legal expansion, either by using existing buildings around the tiny house or by erecting, sometimes hastily, legal annexes. The latter have taken on diverse forms, including the adoption of national implementing legislation, jurisprudential developments, and the creation of soft law (through United Nations General Assembly Resolutions and the Conclusions of the United Nations High Commissioner's Executive Committee). As to "squatting" in existing buildings, refugee law has made use of two sister branches of law: human rights law and international humanitarian law.

The strategy appears simple. Refugee law, emerging from the 1951 Refugee Convention, can make up for the 'gaps', its normative fuzziness and lack of enforcement mechanisms by leaning on other international human rights and humanitarian laws (Gorlick:2000). Thus, the widely ratified human rights treaties - ICERD, ICCPR, ICESCR, CEDAW, CAT and CRC- serve to supplement, if not reinforce, the Refugee Convention. Similarly, international humanitarian law which relates to conduct during conflict offers the 1949 Fourth Geneva Convention Relative to the Protection of Civilian Persons in time of War, which aims to protect civilian victims, deals with refugees and displaced persons (see Article 44). This convention is expanded by the 1977 Additional Protocol which considers refugees and stateless persons as protected persons (Article 73). Though provisions of international humanitarian law, international criminal law, and international human rights law

---

[69] Theo Van Boven, 'Security Council: The New Frontier, The' (1992) 48 ICJ Rev 12
[70] Stephane Jaquemet, 'The Cross-Fertilization of International Humanitarian Law and International Refugee Law' (2001) 83 Revue Internationale de la Croix-Rouge/International Review of the Red Cross 651

are each aimed at different periods of the refugee cycle and actors[71], they serve to provide synergy. The most significant expansion of refugee law through human rights and humanitarian principles, however, has been through the contribution of a variety of players and sources leading to the 'soft law' mentioned above.

There are dangers in construing refugee rights from an exclusively legal or human rights treaty basis. The Convention's human rights methodology is committed to an individualist, largely civil and political rights approach which excludes large categories of forced migrants (as discussed in the chapter on legal definitions). Moreover, refugee rights in the Convention are selective and partial not covering all stages of the refugee cycle. Thus women, children, internally displaced or environmental refugees are ignored. As Bhabha notes

> This [present human rights] system produces benefits for a somewhat arbitrarily selected minority of forced migrants: foreign policy considerations and access to resources, most importantly high quality legal representation, make a dramatic difference to the prospects of success. Thus, while thousands of applicants gain refugee status or some form of subsidiary humanitarian protection, tens of thousands live in a limbo of illegality without access to basic civil rights, or are incarcerated for years as they await a decision on their cases, and hundreds of thousands are rejected, unable to gain access to a forum where the adjudication of refugee protection can be made in the first place. Advocates are scarce and most asylum applications end in failure[72].

While a number of commentators interpret human rights violations (and failure of State protection) to be the basis of refugeehood under the Refugee Convention, the Convention's commitment to an undefined and restrictive concept of "persecution" serves as the exclusive benchmark for refugee status.

There is also considerable discontent over the emphasis on 'individual' rights over a 'collective rights' approach which is of particular significance in systematic human rights violations. Moreover, the rights language, at least in the Convention, seems to be directed at the receiving State, not the host State. Most crucially, the Convention does not address the central question for receiving societies – why it is their responsibility to accept refugees into their fold and why forced migrants are a

---

[71] Liesbeth Zegveld, *Accountability of Armed Opposition Groups in International Law*, vol 24 (Cambridge University Press 2002): 229

[72] Jacqueline Bhabha, 'Internationalist Gatekeepers: The Tension between Asylum Advocacy and Human Rights' (2002) 15 Harv Hum Rts J 155: 161

special category deserving of special protection over other types of migrants. These are not explained by the existence of human rights itself, but rather through human rights contexts. Moreover, rights conceived by State agreements do little to incorporate refugee concerns, choices or provide for refugee 'ownership' of their rights.

If we are indeed living in an 'age of rights'[73] where human rights are 'the new standard of civilisation' by which States are to be held accountable[74], why have refugee rights been so elusive in practice? The debate between universalists (who believe that human rights are applicable the same everywhere and to everyone) and cultural relativists (that human rights to an extent depend on the context and subscribers)[75] has been well documented. The universalists claim that human rights as undisputed because there appears to be general *de facto* international agreement among the States[76]. The term 'cultural relativism' is derived mostly from debates amongst anthropologists (who consider human nature as biological as well as social) and moral philosophers (who often denounce hierarchies and essentialism).

Unlike several other branches of human rights from women's rights to criminal law, the universalist-relativist debate may not be the central issue because the idea of asylum is agreed to be cross-cultural. No State claims that their culture or religion does not support asylum rights, rather the objections are pragmatic. Yet, where human rights are manifested top-down, ahistorically and in isolation from their social, political, and economic milieu, they discount the lived experience and expectations of those outside the 'Western' consciousness[77]. Anker[78] argues that given that international refugee law involves one State's judgment of another, it is inherently a political and conflictual field

While refugee law may be formally non-intrusive and non-judgmental, it does make a determination of a state's willingness and ability to protect a particular citizen or resident, and in so doing lays claim to an *international* human rights standard. When the legalized refugee regime consists almost exclusively of states in the North determining refugee claims from the South, these purportedly

---

[73] Norberto Bobbio and Allan Cameron, 'The Age of Rights' (1997)

[74] Jack Donnelly, 'Human Rights: A New Standard of Civilization?' (1998) 74 International Affairs 1

[75] John J Tilley, 'Cultural Relativism' (2000) 22 Human Rights Quarterly 501

[76] Donnelly, 'Human Rights: A New Standard of Civilization?'

[77] Adamantia Pollis, 'Cultural Relativism Revisited: Through a State Prism' (1996) 18 Human Rights Quarterly 316

[78] Deborah E Anker, 'Refugee Law, Gender, and the Human Rights Paradigm' (2002) 15 Harv Hum Rts J 133: 152

international human rights-based judgments seem one-sided, patronizing, and hypocritical.

Writers like Freeman[79] argue that claims of 'consensus' over human rights are puzzling because they are at best limited. The reluctance to study philosophical foundations of human rights generally, and refugee rights in particular, has been problematic. There is no agreement on whether human rights are derived from divine authority, natural law, or considerations concerning human nature. No single theory of human rights emerges because political scientists, philosophers, historians, international relations experts, politicians, philosophers, lawyers, theologians and anthropologists dispute the foundations and rationale for rights. Can we agree on the goals without concurrence on the sources and the means? Though human rights are set up to 'trump' other arguments, they do not silence the variety of interests in a given society, particularly where societies are hostile or ambivalent towards refugees.

Several writers find the communitarian argument- that moral beliefs of large majorities are binding on dissenting minorities- to be dangerous without shared values. A hierarchical view of values, cultures and social order is likely to lead to conflict. This is particularly true of refugee rights where there are practical issues of State sovereignty, national security and notions of 'membership' of societies. Human rights cannot be conjured by mere academic or legal skill but need to be tested for their validity[80]. For example, even where human rights are widely subscribed, the question as to whether refugees are equal claimants to rights, as nationals, persists. Though human rights are often a convenient language, both supporters of refugee rights, as well as violators/dissenters, do in fact offer moral and other justifications for their positions. The human rights movement thus assumes a rights-based morality, but this must be recognized to be narrower than the range of choices and dimensions that are expressed within societies.

Some commentators suggest that human rights need neither theory or reason, what it required is passion and courage[81]. Since truth is not an absolute, verifiable or objective - particularly in a contested arena such as refugees- the quest for a simple all-encompassing theory of rights is futile. Thus, Rawls (1993) is satisfied that human rights depend neither on a specific moral doctrine, nor on a particular conception of human nature. Rather, 'basic human rights express a minimum

---

[79] Michael Freeman, 'The Philosophical Foundations of Human Rights' (1994) 16 Human Rights Quarterly 491
[80] Philip Alston, 'Conjuring up New Human Rights: A Proposal for Quality Control' (1984) 78 The American Journal of International Law 607
[81] Richard Rorty, 'Human Rights, Rationality, and Sentimentality' (1993)

standard of well-ordered political institutions for all peoples who belong, as members in good standing, to a *just* political society of peoples.'[82]. Yet, human rights as 'interests' are caught up with diverse constituencies and competing goals. As Donnelly[83] points out

Rights are 'interests' that have been specially entrenched in a system of justifications and thereby substantially transformed, giving them priority, in ordinary circumstances, over, for example, utilitarian calculations, mere interests, or considerations of social policy ... which otherwise would be not only appropriate, but decisive, reasons for public or private action.

Thus refugee rights, far from being settled through legal provision or advocacy positions, continually need to be explored as well as canvassed. Competing theories of human rights and responsibilities, which pragmatists may find futile and distracting, serve to underline that human rights, though well meaning, are constructed on debatable foundations. Refugee rights are not merely a problem of devious avoidance or lack of implementation will, they need to be interrogated as regards their form, substance, mode of articulation and their place in the contemporary socio-political world.

## Building Normative Consensus

One of the perceived benefits of a human rights approach to the refugee issues comes from standard setting, promotion of refugee protection and in clarifying the obligations of States as well as other stakeholders. Refugee protection norms are generated by a host of international, regional and State. For example, the six main human rights treaty bodies adopt 'general comments' akin to the normative standards adopted by the UNHCR's Executive Committee of the High Commissioner's Programme (EXCOM) and the Department of International Protection ('DIP') which though not formally binding, remain influential[84]. However, this enterprise of filling in the gaps and responding to refugee experiences has been challenging, as demonstrated by the efforts to elucidate even the most fundamental of the refugee doctrines, the principle of *non-refoulement*.

According to article 33, paragraph 1 of the Refugee Convention 'No Contracting State shall expel or return (*"refouler "*) a refugee in any manner whatsoever to the

---

[82] John Rawls, 'The Law of Peoples' (1993) 20 Critical Inquiry 36

[83] Jack Donnelly, 'Universal Human Rights in Theory and Practice' (2003) Ithaca, New York1989, 112ff

[84] Guy Goodwin-Gill and David Petrasek, 'The 44th Session of the Unhcr Executive Committee: A View from the Side' (1994) 6 International Journal of Refugee Law 63

frontiers of territories where his life or freedom would be threatened on account of his race, religion, nationality, membership of a particular social group or political opinion'. Arulananthan, like others, considers the doctrine as the lynch pin of refugee protection[85]

*(Non-refoulement)* shows do not always act exclusively in their narrow self-interest. If they did, they would simply refuse to take nearly all refugees. However, the fact that, in most cases, states refuse to return refugees to their home countries, and that when they do return refugees they do so in covert ways rather than openly admitting it while denying the practice, shows that the norm of refugee protection can be effective in a politically viable system of refugee protection.

*Non-refoulement* is a broad principle, which includes non-return, and non-rejection at the frontier and is relevant to the politics of *non-entrée* on refugee protection. However, consider the debate over its nature and scope. Chimni outlines how three eminent refugee law experts Hathaway, Goodwin-Gill, and Hailbronner take different positions. Goodwin Gill argues that *non-refoulement* is not merely a Convention principle and owing to its customary status can be extended to non-Convention refugees while Hailbronner is against such a proposition and Hathaway 'aspires to occupy middle ground'[86]. Some would argue that *non-refoulement* is a peremptory norm or *jus cogens* that is a high-ranking legal principle [87], others would be more cautious as to its practical utility. Beyond theorizing *non-refoulement*, its application serves to demonstrate the difficulty in getting human rights approaches to work for refugees.

States have long seized on the fact that *non-refoulement* is not an absolute right under Article 33. It can be suspended if there are reasonable grounds for regarding the asylum-seeker as a danger to the security of the host country, or if the asylum-seeker has been convicted of "a particularly serious crime" and constitutes a danger to the host country. This is contrary to the conception of *non-refoulement* under Article 3 of the European Convention on Human Rights, Article 7 of the International Covenant on Civil and Political Rights and Article 3 of the Convention against Torture where it is absolute. No exceptions and no derogations are permitted, not even if an alleged terrorist constitutes a danger to the national security of a country[88].

---

[85] Ahilan T Arulanantham, 'Restructured Safe Havens: A Proposal for Reform of the Refugee Protection System' (2000) 22 Human Rights Quarterly 1: 5

[86] Bhupinder Singh Chimni, *International Refugee Law: A Reader* (SAGE Publications Pvt. Limited 2000): 86

[87] Jean Allain, 'The Jus Cogens Nature of Non-Refoulement' (2001) 13 International Journal of Refugee Law 533

[88] Alberta Fabbricotti, 'The Concept of Inhuman or Degrading Treatment in International Law and Its Application in Asylum Cases' (1998) 10 International

Even before 9/11, the *MV Tampa* case showed how States could circumvent their *non-refoulement* obligations, even where there was no determined security threat[89]. The 433 asylum seekers, travelling from Indonesia, on the Norwegian-registered *MV Tampa* were denied permission to land in Australia before being taken to Nauru and New Zealand, in order to have their asylum claims processed. Several countries including Australia and the United States of America consider *non-refoulement* to be applicable only if the refugee physically succeeds in reaching their territory. As such, States regularly use pre-entry controls and interception of refugees as valid devices to frustrate refugee access to their territory. The Convention being ambiguous or silent on vital issues, States are able to do what they want and claim, as Australia did in this case, that there was no Convention violation owing to the refugee interception. Schloenhardt[90] argues that the introduction of mandatory detention of unauthorised arrivals in particular marked the beginning of a gradual slide into a policy of 'deterrence, detention and denial' by systematically discriminatory against asylum seekers.

International refugee law faces its sternest test as the "war against terror" continues[91]. National security clauses have been increasingly invoked by States to *refoule* asylum seekers on grounds of suspected terrorism. A spate of legislations post 9/11 in different parts of the world (and 7/7 2005 in the UK) provide for a terrorism-suspect-exception to asylum. Despite the Refugee Convention already possessing sufficient inbuilt provisions to exclude terrorists from the benefits of the convention- (See Article 1F of the Refugee Convention), the post 9/11 developments have fuelled a backlash against refugees – and specific categories of migrants - across the world.

Although none of the 11 September hijackers entered the US as refugees, for a media and government that rely on simple messages of fear, any Arab or Muslim is suspect. Racial profiling, discredited in US policing, has made a comeback. 'Driving while black' is replaced by 'flying while Arab' as the trigger for a pre-emptive detention by police or immigration authorities. If the general climate of suspicion and racism is not hazardous enough, for many asylum seekers the 'war on terrorism' poses particular dangers[92].

---

journal of refugee law International journal of refugee law 637

[89] Tara Magner, 'A Less Than 'Pacific' Solution for Asylum Seekers in Australia' (2004) 16 International Journal of Refugee Law 53

[90] Andreas Schloenhardt, 'To Deter, Detain and Deny : Protection of Onshore Asylum Seekers in Australia' (2002) 14 International journal of refugee law International journal of refugee law 302

[91] Siraj Sait, 'International Refugee Law: Excluding the Palestinians' (2002) Law After Ground Zero 11

There has been a perceptible change in the thrust of UN resolutions which now discard the reminder to States to balance their anti-terror efforts with respect for the 1951 Refugee Convention. It calls on States to ensure that "that the asylum seeker has not planned, facilitated or participated in the commission of terrorists acts" or that "refugee status is not abused by perpetrators, organisers or facilitators of terrorist acts" (UN Security Council Resolution 1373, 28 September 2001). From the USA-PATRIOT Act 2001 to the UK Anti-Terrorism, Crime and Security Act 2001, asylum seeking has been made more difficult with individuals penalized merely due their origin in a country of conflict with tenuous political, ethnic or religious affiliations or ties to discredited organisations.

In addition, the curtailing of welfare benefits for refugees has led to destitution, in violation of their basic human rights[93]. The war against terror provides cover for States to target the most vulnerable and needy of protection- the refugees. Though the potential use of the asylum channel by terrorists is no doubt real, States have failed to seriously develop a system of considering the dangers faced by those excluded from the States' post 9/11 summary refugee exclusion policies[94]. A number of European ideas such as the 2003 UK proposal for 'regional protection areas' in locations close to countries that produce significant numbers of refugees and asylum seekers fail to recognize basic principles of refugee rights law. Curtis' comment in a broader context that 'violating international law has become as British as afternoon tea'[95], has assumed ominous portents for State responses to refugee flows.

## Enforcing Refugee Rights

Violation of Convention refugee rights, in theory, entails State 'responsibility' whereby the State would be held accountable under international[96]. While refugee rights have been promoted by a range of refugee support groups, the limited opportunities to secure their enforcement, particularly in the face of hostile governmental policies, are all too apparent. The problem begins with the lack of monitoring provisions within the 1951 Refugee Convention deferring to the State the

---

[92] D Lawson, 'Refugee! Terrorist! Criminal!' (2002) 350 New Internationalist 24
[93] Ryszard Cholewinski, 'Enforced Destitution of Asylum Seekers in the United Kingdom : The Denial of Fundamental Human Rights' (1998) 10 International journal of refugee law International journal of refugee law 462
[94] Edward Newman and Joanne Van Selm, 'Refugees and Forced Displacement : International Security, Human Vulnerability, and the State' (2003): 10
[95] Mark Curtis, *Web of Deceit : Britain's Real Role in the World* (Vintage 2003)
[96] Chaloka Beyani, 'State Responsibility for the Prevention and Resolution of Forced Population Displacements in International Law' (1995) 1995/special International journal of refugee law 130; Naomi Roht-Arriaza, 'Impunity and Human Rights in International Law and Practice' (1995)

adoption of refugee policies that are rights compliant. But there is no effective international monitoring of the same. Article 35(1) of the Refugee Convention does hold out a potential for international supervision of State refugee policies

The Contracting States undertake to co-operate with UNHCR, or any other agency of the United Nations which may succeed it, in the exercise of its functions, and shall in particular facilitate its duty of supervising the application of the provisions of this Convention.

Yet, there has never been a serious consideration of how the UNHCR, primarily a humanitarian agency promoting refugee rights mandate with a limited protection mandate secured through 'good offices', can fit into this active monitoring role[97]. As Gilbert[98] points out, despite the expanded role of UNHCR, it is still governed by its 1950 mandate which inhibits its expanded role and its response to contemporary challenges. Despite its efforts to appear above the politics, the UNHCR is inevitably drawn into it[99]. In 2001, UNHCR initiated the Global Consultations on International Protection on three 'tracks'- to strengthen State commitments to the 1951 Refugee Convention and the 1967 protocol, to facilitate positive interpretations of disputed notions in light of current developments, and to review protection policy matters which address contemporary challenges[100]. UNHCR's role and achievements as the primary global refugee agency have been generally noteworthy but its financial dependence on a handful of Western donors has forced it to be nuanced in its assertion of refugee rights[101].

The United Nations has been preoccupied generally with issues of international peace and security, with refugee issues being at best a peripheral concern or part of

---

[97] Walter Kälin, 'Supervising the 1951 Convention Relating to the Status of Refugees : Article 35 and Beyond' (2003) Refugee protection in international law : UNHCR's global consultations on international protection Refugee Protection in International Law : UNHCR's Global Consultations on International Protection / ed by Erika Feller, Volker Türk and Frances Nicholson, ISBN 0521532817 613

[98] G. Gilbert, 'Rights, Legitimate Expectations, Needs and Responsibilities: Unhcr and the New World Order' (1998) 10 INTERNATIONAL JOURNAL OF REFUGEE LAW 349

[99] David P. Forsythe and others, *Unhcr's Mandate : The Politics of Being Non-Political* (UNHCR 2001)

[100] Erika Feller, Volker Türk and Frances Nicholson, *Refugee Protection in International Law: Unhcr's Global Consultations on International Protection* (Cambridge University Press 2003)

[101] Gil Loescher, *The Unhcr and World Politics : A Perilous Path* (Oxford University Press 2001); Michael Barutciski, 'A Critical View on Unhcr's Mandate Dilemmas' (2002) 14 International journal of refugee law International journal of refugee law 365

the stability question. Intervening in refugee crisis in sovereign states has been tricky which contentious issues as to who decides when to intervene (and following what rules of procedure and evidence) and what the appropriate response should be?[102] The few interventions in the name of refugees have focused on the immediate humanitarian crisis, rather than addressing the root causes of the refugee movement[103]. As a result, the current refugee containment policies from a humanitarian rather than a rights-based approach have resulted, in part, to more than half of the world refugee population being warehoused in camps deprived of basic rights, in situations lasting 10 years or more. It also supports the dismal view that human rights may be able to deal with the trickle of refugee cases but breaks down in cases of mass refugee influx, demonstrating the virtual irrelevance of the human rights project in some contexts.

The increasing interest of UN human rights system - the Charter based bodies such as the Human Rights Commission and its sub-commission (now the Human Rights Council), the thematic and country rapporteurs and particularly the committees supervising the six main human rights treaties – in refugee rights has been significant. The Human Rights Committee (supervising the ICCPR) and the Committee against Torture, who have an individual complaints system with respect to States who have agreed to it, have the experience of handling asylum cases directly. However, most of the international refugee rights material supervision (from the six treaties) is based primarily on exchanges within committees following States submission of periodic reports detailing implementation under each convention (see Steiner)[104]. The prospects for 'enforcement', however, are virtually non-existent. The best that these human rights bodies can hope for is to 'name and shame' the serial offending States, with the orchestration of the refugee support groups. But with 'best practice' scarce among countries regarding refugee policies, publicity for refugee rights violations can hardly be a deterrent or persuasive unless it is converted into a human rights campaign nationally.

Effective international refugee protection is no doubt an important goal, but it is after all surrogate to national protection- resulting from the failure of the state to

---

[102] Albrecht Schnabel and Ramesh Chandra Thakur, *Kosovo and the Challenge of Humanitarian Intervention: Selective Indignation, Collective Action, and International Citizenship* (United Nations University Press 2000); Chimni, *International Refugee Law: A Reader*

[103] Alan Dowty and Gil Loescher, 'Refugee Flows as Grounds for International Action' (1996) International security 43

[104] Henry J. Steiner, 'Individual Claims in a World of Massive Violations : What Role for the Human Rights Committee?' (2000) The future of UN human rights treaty monitoring / edited by Philip Alston and James Crawford

protect human rights. In some countries, constitutional provisions or the existence of a strong regional human rights system provides opportunities for effective remedies. The European Convention of Human Rights with its freedom against torture (Article 3) provides an example of how asylum seekers can use human rights procedures effectively[105]. Starting from the *Soering* case (1989), the European Court of Human Rights has stressed the extraterritorial construction of human rights responsibility, whereby a State would have to consider the implications of its deportation, expulsion or extradition decision. The absolute prohibition on torture applies irrespective of the activities of the individual in question, however undesirable or dangerous (Ahmed v Australia 1996), could apply to threat of persecution from non-State actors and in specific circumstances where the deported person's health may be directly affected (See D v UK 1997). Procedural rights, family reunion, non-discrimination as well as issues such as safe third country and detention have been subject to judicial review (See Blake and Fransman)[106]. Yet, Europe sees an intense competition between expanding application of human rights to refugees and the restrictive 'fortress Europe' trends which seek to restrict avenues for seeking asylum.

The role of judicial review by national judges is critical to giving life to human rights but there is a tendency of national courts to avoid international law issues[107]. One of the sites where refugee rights are being vigorously contested is at the national courts, where refugees have scored some impressive gains as well as suffered some setbacks. While the separation of powers doctrine and limits of judicial review in specific Constitutional schemes may be relevant, access to justice for the refugees has been unpredictable. Judges are not politically insulated or able to resist stereotypes about refugees. Legomsky, comparing British and American judges, argues that "factors other than legal reasoning" in immigration judicial decision making may be relevant. He cites "backgrounds, attitudes and role perceptions of individual judges, and the contemporary political forces prevailing in society".[108]

---

[105] Hélène Lambert, 'Protection against Refoulement from Europe: Human Rights Law Comes to the Rescue' (1999) 48 ICLQ 515

[106] Nicholas J. Blake, Laurie Fransman and Chambers Two Garden Court, *Immigration, Nationality, and Asylum under the Human Rights Act 1998* (Butterworths 1999)

[107] Rosalyn Higgins, *Problems and Process : International Law and How We Use It* (Clarendon Press ; Oxford University Press 1994)

[108] Stephen H. Legomsky, *Immigration and the Judiciary : Law and Politics in Britain and America* (Clarendon Press ; Oxford University Press 1987): 223

The Canadian Supreme Court case of *Suresh* (2002) points to the dilemmas courts face in dealing with international refugee principles. In this case, the scope of *non-refoulement* in deportation proceedings was in question. Suresh, an asylum seeker from Sri Lanka, faced deportation since he was found to be a member of the Tamil Tigers (LTTE), classified as a terrorist organisation. In ordering fresh deportation hearings, the Court held that deportation must be based on full facts but that deportation can take place even if there was a chance of torture on deportation. The positive reading of the Suresh case was that deportation decisions involving *non-refoulement* were to be decided in the context of fair procedure and human rights standards[109]. But it also demonstrates the trade-offs that are continually made between asylum rights and security and other interests.

Human rights campaigners have been deeply concerned about torture being viewed 'as something that can be balanced away by a national security risk – one that is thus unsatisfactory from an international human rights perspective'[110]. As Weiner notes, there are five broad categories in which refugees or migrants may be perceived as either a threat or a benefit to the sending country, to the receiving country, or to relations between the two[111]. The reality is that it is such perception, in turn, which determines State willingness to respect the principle of *non-refoulement* and refugee rights. Human rights, however, bounce back where the scales have been seriously tipped, like the UK House of Lords case over the Belmarsh detainees where indefinite detention and forced confessions have been held unlawful. Human rights of refugees are not about broad general aspirational principles as promoted formally but whether they are accessible to refugees who need them. Human rights is about power, legitimacy and authority but equally about interests and social values in each society.

## Proposals For International Refugee Protection

The dominant theme in refugee discourse today is how, not whether, to reform the international regime[112]. A range of 'workable' proposals or arrangements, which challenge the assumptions and principles that have long driving international

---

[109] Gerald P. Heckman, 'Securing Procedural Safeguards for Asylum Seekers in Canadian Law : An Expanding Role for International Human Rights Law' (2003) 15 International journal of refugee law International journal of refugee law 212

[110] Obiora Chinedu Okafor and Pius Lekwuwa Okoronkwo, 'Reconfiguring Nonrefoulement? The Suresh Decision, Security Relativism, and the International Human Rights Imperative' (2003) 15 International Journal of Refugee Law 30

[111] Myron Weiner, 'Security, Stability, and International Migration' (1992) International security 91: 105

[112] Bimal Ghosh, *Managing Migration : Time for a New International Regime?* (Oxford University Press 2000)

refugee policies, are being vigorously canvassed. For the UNHCR, a pragmatic strategy has been to supplement the Refugee Convention with supplemental State obligations as part of the 'Convention Plus' strategy. The vexing question, however, is how to get States to take their obligations seriously, given their anxiety over the number of asylum seekers and the perceived threat of refugees to the receiving society. For a number of refugee writers, this can be done only by responding to State concerns and interests and respecting State sovereignty, their right to control their borders and their willingness and ability to absorb forced migrants. Others argue that forced migrants are recognized as a special category that ought to be treated by States in accordance with international law and humanitarian principles. At the centre of the debate is the clash between State interests and refugee rights.

Crisp rightly points the international community cannot succeed unless it is proactively willing to focus on the state producing the refugee flow, not only on the State accepting displaced persons[113]. Western States complain (speciously) that they are absorbing a disproportionate share of refugees and the central question is one of burden sharing. Human rights monitoring, modest as it is, is the only way of creating a proactive mechanism where conditions of persecution can be addressed. However, refugee solutions – though ideally based on return to safety and security in countries of origin- inevitably involve the ability of other States to provide an adoptive home to refugees. One of the influential theories in Western circles is the idea of a contrived collectivized solution on the basis of "differentiated responsibility among states"[114].

The 'differentiated responsibility' approach is based on the premise that (Western) refugee receiving States need not 'settle' refugees they receive, as long as they are able to find alternative solutions that offer refugee protection - elsewhere. Hathaway's argument has been that the Refugee Convention never explicitly required a state to provide permanent residence to those seeking asylum in its territory, merely an obligation not to *refoule* to a country where the asylum seeker may face persecution[115]. He points to Article 34 of the Refugee Convention which merely requires that assimilation and naturalisation of refugees be done as "far as possible". Schuck carries this framework further, seeking burden sharing through quotas with the option to pay other States to take over obligations[116]. The building

---

[113] Jeff Crisp, *A New Asylum Paradigm?: Globalization, Migration and the Uncertain Future of the International Refugee Regime* (United nations High commissioner for refugees (UNHCR) 2003)

[114] J Hathaway and A Neve, 'Making International Law Relevant Again: A Proposal for Collectivized Solution-Orientated Protection' (1997) 10 Harv Hum Rts J 115

[115] Ibid 2

[116] Peter H Schuck, 'Refugee Burden-Sharing: A Modest Proposal' (1997) 22 Yale J

blocks for this scheme, which recognises the positions and 'absorptive capacity' of States, are burden sharing through negotiation, temporary protection, safe havens and ultimately repatriation.

Temporary protection[117] has been offered as a realist solution based on the advantages of quick (temporary) asylum decisions, improvement in the 'quality' of asylum and certainty for asylum to make alternate plans for repatriation, or for resettlement in a third state within a certain timeframe. However, the proposal essentially exchanges the existing assortment of limited State driven Convention obligations with a degraded set of State centred expectations, decentring the refugee even further. Anker, Fitzpatrick and Shacknove, in a direct rebuttal of these proposals, fear that asylum-seekers "would largely be removed from the realm of law and consigned to the realm of political bargaining" leading to the "commodification" of refugees[118]. They argue that institutional protection of the human rights of refugees, not collectivised political solutions, should determine refugee policies.

The debate over what minimum obligations receiving States should have towards those fleeing persecution stands in sharp contrast to the recent Latin American position. Twenty Latin American Countries, in November 2004, adopted the Mexico Refugee Action Plan aimed at refugee protection not on the basis of burden sharing, but in the spirit of "solidarity between neighbours". International refugee principles remain the same, but the 'spirit' in which they are applied varies. As Juss[119] points out, reform of refugee law can be morally legitimate only where refugee rights rather than national self-interest are the markers. The reality is that negotiations over the future international framework are being driven by States rather than refugee lobbies but though refugee rights are being resisted as the primary criteria for reform, rights-based approaches are a fundamental component.

## Conclusion

No doubt human rights now occupy a high profile in the refugee discourse, both as standards of expectation as well as a narrative of State failings. Refugee lawyers, adjudicators and the civil society increasingly use laws, reports and testimonies to

---

Int'l L 243

[117] Joan Fitzpatrick, 'Temporary Protection of Refugees: Elements of a Formalized Regime' (2000) American Journal of International Law 279

[118] Deborah Anker, Joan Fitzpatrick and Andrew Shacknove, 'Crisis and Cure: A Reply to Hathaway/Neve and Schuck' (1998) 11 Harv Hum Rts J 295

[119] Satvinder Singh Juss, 'Toward a Morally Legitimate Reform of Refugee Law : The Use of Cultural Jurisprudence' (1998) 11 Harvard human rights journal 311

monitor refugee rights but whether the promise of human rights has been substantially delivered – to a tangible proportion of displaced - is still contested. Oona Hathaway[120] doubts whether the mere signing up of human rights treaties translates into better human rights records. Analysing a database of 166 nations over a nearly forty-year period in five areas of human rights law, Hathaway finds that States often ratify treaties as a means of deflecting internal or external pressure for real change, and countries with dismal human rights record often calculate that treaty ratification would be a shield from international scrutiny. Neumayer[121], on the other hand, finds that though treaty ratification rarely has unconditional effects on human rights, it generally does improve respect for human rights, conditional on the extent of democracy and the strength of civil society. He adds

> "For treaty ratification to work, there must be conditions for domestic groups, parties, and individuals and for civil society to persuade, convince, and perhaps pressure governments into translating the formal promise of better human rights protection into actual reality"[122].

Refugee rights, however, cannot merely be provisions from the Refugee Convention or human rights treaties. Such over formalisation is limiting since the human rights legal conceptualization, as discussed above, appears to cater only to certain rights, particular categories of forced migrants and selective stages of the refugee cycle. Women, children and the internally displaced, for example, have been generally side-lined. Human rights are neither the preserve of the law nor the State- though these are often the frames- but instead dwell in the dynamic rhetoric and activism of refugees and refugee advocates. The challenge for refugee rights is precisely its conversion into a refugee led counterbalance for State power and discretion, rather than a State soliloquy of trade-offs. For the refugee rights framework to have the capacity offer meaningful and consistent refugee protection, it is not the international naming and shaming, but the willingness as well as the institutional capacities of States to recognize those rights that matters.

Conceiving human rights as mere aspirations of societies has been easier than creating consistent and robust refugee protection guarantees. Refugee rights experience the same problems of deficient monitoring, compliance and enforcement mechanism as do other human rights. Yet, their formulation is even more fragile

---

[120] Oona A Hathaway 'Do Human Rights Treaties Make a Difference?' (2002) 111 The Yale Law Journal 1935
[121] Eric Neumayer, 'Do International Human Rights Treaties Improve Respect for Human Rights?' (2005) 49 Journal of conflict resolution 925
[122] Ibid 953

because refugees, displaced by their own State, are not yet considered equal members in the receiving country nor do they have the support systems. Moreover, refugee rights are often contingent on the manner of their entry and ultimately the 'refugee status' determination, and asylum rights are rather fluid. And while individual cases are manageable, human rights are often the first causality in challenging contexts such as conflicts, mass influx and xenophobia.

Even though refugee rights are a potentially powerful strategy in refugee protection, their materialization into tangible material benefits would depend on a variety of factors. Refugee rights need to be further grounded in the shared values and interests of society, stimulate refugee centeredness and participation, mainstreamed through the involvement of all stakeholders and above all be seen by all States as the new 'standard of civilisation'. For both the idealist and the cynic writing the definitive opinion on whether refugee rights works, it is best to be reminded that refugee rights is a relatively new development and, as a movement, still in its infancy. But can the millions of refugees worldwide, being deprived of their basic rights every day, afford to wait for the sight of the promised land of rights.

# References

Bayefsky AF, United Nations Human Rights Treaty System: Universality at the Crossroads (Martinus Nijhoff Publishers 2001)

Blake NJ, Fransman L and Two Garden Court C, Immigration, Nationality, and Asylum under the Human Rights Act 1998 (Butterworths 1999)

Chimni BS, *International Refugee Law: A Reader* (SAGE Publications Pvt. Limited 2000)

Crisp J, A New Asylum Paradigm?: Globalization, Migration and the Uncertain Future of the International Refugee Regime (United nations High commissioner for refugees (UNHCR) 2003)

Curtis M, Web of Deceit : Britain's Real Role in the World (Vintage 2003)

Feller E, Türk V and Nicholson F, Refugee Protection in International Law: Unhcr's Global Consultations on International Protection (Cambridge University Press 2003)

Forsythe DP and others, Unhcr's Mandate : The Politics of Being Non-Political (UNHCR 2001)

Ghosh B, Managing Migration : Time for a New International Regime? (Oxford University Press 2000)

Higgins R, *Problems and Process : International Law and How We Use It* (Clarendon Press ; Oxford University Press 1994)

Legomsky SH, Immigration and the Judiciary : Law and Politics in Britain and America (Clarendon Press ; Oxford University Press 1987)

Loescher G, The Unhcr and World Politics : A Perilous Path (Oxford University Press 2001)

Nicholson F and Twomey PM, *Refugee Rights and Realities: Evolving International Concepts and Regimes* (Cambridge University Press Cambridge, UK 1999)

Schnabel A and Thakur RC, Kosovo and the Challenge of Humanitarian Intervention: Selective Indignation, Collective Action, and International Citizenship (United Nations University Press 2000)

Tuitt P, False Images: Law's Construction of the Refugee (Pluto Pr 1996)

Zegveld L, Accountability of Armed Opposition Groups in International Law, vol 24 (Cambridge University Press 2002)

United Nations High Commissioner for Refugees, The State of the World's Refugees 2006: Human Displacement in the New Millennium (2006)

Allain J, 'The Jus Cogens Nature of Non-Refoulement' (2001) 13 International Journal of Refugee Law 533

Alston P, 'Conjuring up New Human Rights: A Proposal for Quality Control' (1984) 78 The American Journal of International Law 607

Anker D, Fitzpatrick J and Shacknove A, 'Crisis and Cure: A Reply to Hathaway/Neve and Schuck' (1998) 11 Harv Hum Rts J 295

Anker DE, 'Refugee Law, Gender, and the Human Rights Paradigm' (2002) 15 Harv Hum Rts J 133

Arulanantham AT, 'Restructured Safe Havens: A Proposal for Reform of the Refugee Protection System' (2000) 22 Human Rights Quarterly 1

Barutciski M, 'A Critical View on Unhcr's Mandate Dilemmas' (2002) 14 International journal of refugee law International journal of refugee law 365

Beyani C, 'State Responsibility for the Prevention and Resolution of Forced Population Displacements in International Law' (1995) 1995/special International journal of refugee law 130

Bhabha J, 'Internationalist Gatekeepers: The Tension between Asylum Advocacy and Human Rights' (2002) 15 Harv Hum Rts J 155

Bobbio N and Cameron A, 'The Age of Rights' (1997)

Cholewinski R, 'Enforced Destitution of Asylum Seekers in the United Kingdom : The Denial of Fundamental Human Rights' (1998) 10 International journal of refugee law International journal of refugee law 462

Donnelly J, 'Human Rights: A New Standard of Civilization?' (1998) 74 International Affairs 1

Donnelly J, 'Universal Human Rights in Theory and Practice' (2003) Ithaca, New York1989, 112ff

Dowty A and Loescher G, 'Refugee Flows as Grounds for International Action' (1996) International security 43

Edwards A, 'Human Rights, Refugees, and the Right 'to Enjoy'asylum' (2005) 17 International Journal of Refugee Law 293

Fabbricotti A, 'The Concept of Inhuman or Degrading Treatment in International Law and Its Application in Asylum Cases' (1998) 10 International journal of refugee law International journal of refugee law 637

Fitzpatrick J, 'Temporary Protection of Refugees: Elements of a Formalized Regime' (2000) American Journal of International Law 279

Freeman M, 'The Philosophical Foundations of Human Rights' (1994) 16 Human Rights Quarterly 491

Gilbert G, 'Rights, Legitimate Expectations, Needs and Responsibilities: Unhcr and the New World Order' (1998) 10 INTERNATIONAL JOURNAL OF REFUGEE LAW 349

Goodwin-Gill G and Petrasek D, 'The 44th Session of the Unhcr Executive Committee: A View from the Side' (1994) 6 International Journal of Refugee Law 63

Gorlick B, 'Human Rights and Refugees: Enhancing Protection through International Human Rights Law' (2000) 69 Nordic Journal of International Law 117

Hathaway J and Neve A, 'Making International Law Relevant Again: A Proposal for Collectivized Solution-Orientated Protection' (1997) 10 Harv Hum Rts J 115

Hathaway OA, 'Do Human Rights Treaties Make a Difference?' (2002) 111 The Yale Law Journal 1935

Heckman GP, 'Securing Procedural Safeguards for Asylum Seekers in Canadian Law : An Expanding Role for International Human Rights Law' (2003) 15 International journal of refugee law International journal of refugee law 212

Jaquemet S, 'The Cross-Fertilization of International Humanitarian Law and International Refugee Law' (2001) 83 Revue Internationale de la Croix-Rouge/International Review of the Red Cross 651

Juss SS, 'Toward a Morally Legitimate Reform of Refugee Law : The Use of Cultural Jurisprudence' (1998) 11 Harvard human rights journal 311

Kälin W, 'Supervising the 1951 Convention Relating to the Status of Refugees : Article 35 and Beyond' (2003) Refugee protection in international law : UNHCR's global consultations on international protection Refugee Protection in International Law : UNHCR's Global Consultations on International Protection / ed by Erika Feller, Volker Türk and Frances Nicholson, ISBN 0521532817 613

Lambert H, 'Protection against Refoulement from Europe: Human Rights Law Comes to the Rescue' (1999) 48 ICLQ 515

Lawson D, 'Refugee! Terrorist! Criminal!' (2002) 350 New Internationalist 24

Magner T, 'A Less Than 'Pacific' Solution for Asylum Seekers in Australia' (2004) 16 International Journal of Refugee Law 53

Neumayer E, 'Do International Human Rights Treaties Improve Respect for Human Rights?' (2005) 49 Journal of conflict resolution 925

Newman E and Selm Jv, 'Refugees and Forced Displacement : International Security, Human Vulnerability, and the State' (2003)

Okafor OC and Okoronkwo PL, 'Reconfiguring Nonrefoulement? The Suresh Decision, Security Relativism, and the International Human Rights Imperative' (2003) 15 International Journal of Refugee Law 30

Parrish MJ, 'Redefining the Refugee: The Universal Declaration of Human Rights as a Basis for Refugee Protection' (2000) 22 Cardozo L Rev 223

Pollis A, 'Cultural Relativism Revisited: Through a State Prism' (1996) 18 Human Rights Quarterly 316

Rawls J, 'The Law of Peoples' (1993) 20 Critical Inquiry 36

Roht-Arriaza N, 'Impunity and Human Rights in International Law and Practice' (1995)

Rorty R, 'Human Rights, Rationality, and Sentimentality' (1993)

Sait S, 'International Refugee Law: Excluding the Palestinians' (2002) Law After Ground Zero 11

Schloenhardt A, 'To Deter, Detain and Deny : Protection of Onshore Asylum Seekers in Australia' (2002) 14 International journal of refugee law International journal of refugee law 302

Schuck PH, 'Refugee Burden-Sharing: A Modest Proposal' (1997) 22 Yale J Int'l L 243

Steiner HJ, 'Individual Claims in a World of Massive Violations : What Role for the Human Rights Committee?' (2000) The future of UN human rights treaty monitoring / edited by Philip Alston and James Crawford

Tilley JJ, 'Cultural Relativism' (2000) 22 Human Rights Quarterly 501

Van Boven T, 'Security Council: The New Frontier, The' (1992) 48 ICJ Rev 12

Weiner M, 'Security, Stability, and International Migration' (1992) International security 91

# The Battle For Ownership And The Future Of Refugee Law

## M Siraj Sait

*International law proposes certain international norms or standards of treatment or protection for refugees that States are expected to adhere to. In particular, international refugee law provides States legal criteria by which refugees are to be defined and their asylum claims evaluated. However, refugee law is a contested domain and a site of struggle between ideas about of refugee rights and States' attempts to exclude. Law is seen as a formal expression (or camouflage) of State power. It is through legal structures that the most audacious attempts to construct, represent and regulate the refugee phenomenon by States take place. Yet law is also the medium through which the State commits itself to limitations and accountability of its prerogatives and discretions. Despite the intrinsic limitations of law, legal opportunities are often valuable for refugees seeking to enhance their protection. At the centre of the debate over the future shape of refugee law is the battle over who owns it- the State, the refugees or some fictitious international order.*

Law is often deployed within the international refugee discourse as an attempt to trump other arguments relating to refugees. When the term 'law' is used within the refugee discourse, it can signify a particular interest, choice or perspective drawn from a range of legal or quasi-legal sources. Law as a field has almost no boundaries and often contains references to formal documents such as legislation, executive rules, practice guidelines, court decisions or policy papers as well less formal sources. Alternately, refugees may choose to rely on particular formal manifestations of the refugee discourse as authoritative reference points for their advocacy position promoting equitable treatment of displaced persons. Law provides a formal and conventional channel through which reasoning and power must be managed and refugee policies can be challenged. It could provide a bulwark against runaway hostile or racist agendas - subject, of course, to the ability of law to resist those forces. International law assumes certain general principles but rests on national or local legal cultures, contexts and capacities. International refugee law emphasises exceptionalism; but the nexus between asylum and general migration movements makes the promotion of this finer point, for most, difficult in practice [123].

This chapter explores the nature and scope of international law relating to refugees, reviews the 1951 United Nations Convention on the Status of Refugees (hereafter the 1951 Convention) and considers the impact of legal definitions. Exploring the dynamics of international refugee law is indispensable in recognising the potential and the limits of law's empire as well as locating human rights responses and newer models of protection which are discussed in chapter 1.

## The Statist Paradigm Of International Refugee Law

For the refugee who has lost the protection of his or her country or origin, 'the loss of home and political status becomes identical with expulsion from humanity altogether' [124]. This deficit arises from inceptions of classical international law which allocates to each State an exclusive relationship with its own nationals- the concept of sovereignty effectively barring another State's interference. The State system since the Treaty of Westphalia 1648 has significant implications for refugees [125]. In this artificial construct of territorial boundaries and units' refugees fall "between the cracks" of international law's assumed protection theories [126]. They are not only legal anomaly but also a consequence of international law's fiction of neat national-citizen categories. In losing the protective cover of their own States, refugees become voiceless 'pariahs' who must endure the policies of those States who may receive them [127]. International law only partially contends and compensates for their original loss of protection.

International law is State-centric owing to the manner in which law is created. It is the consent of the State through treaties, customs and State practice which is the primary source for international refugee law and the basis for its implementation. One of the characteristics of international refugee law is that it is reflective of a

---

[123] United Nations High Commissioner for Refugees, *The State of the World's Refugees 2006: Human Displacement in the New Millennium* (2006):

[124] Hannah Arendt, *The Origins of Totalitarianism* (New York: Harcourt Brace 1951):

[125] Laura Barnett, 'Global Governance and the Evolution of the International Refugee Regime' (2002) 14 International Journal of Refugee Law 238

[126] Emma Haddad, 'The Refugee: The Individual between Sovereigns' (2003) 17 Global Society 297

[127] Julie Mertus, 'The State and the Post-Cold War Refugee Regime: New Models, New Questions' (1998) 10 International Journal of Refugee Law 321

broad State consensus and 'soft' laws which defer to the State. In general, it does not entertain ethical and moral claims. This is because law and morals are often seen as "two distinct sets of norms that ought to be distinguished... law is a sanctioning order" [128]. This approach creates a serious obstacle in dealing with refugee situations as well as problems of rights. States do not grant refugee status on purely ethical grounds but out of a range of interests and contexts [129]. Recent proposals, discussed in chapter 9, to reform international refugee law are generally preoccupied with State interests in an effort to make refugee protection more palatable to States. International law's attempts to depoliticise itself through the dual step of norm generation and a statement on obligation of States, marginalises its effectiveness in real situations. Refugee issues cannot be sterilized and 'in the long run the international community needs to address the political conditions that lead to refugee movements in the first place' [130].

International law is premised on the agency of the State. It represents the sum total of the State's commitments to the rule of law and investments in the integrity of its processes. Hathaway argues that '[R]efugee law is designed to interpose the protection of the international community only in situations where there is no reasonable expectation that adequate national protection of core human rights will be forthcoming. Refugee law is therefore 'substitute protection' [131]. International refugee protection is therefore not the first port of call for the refugee-rather this is the State. Refugee law offers protection as a surrogate to national protection. The endeavour of international refugee law is to gain consensus on certain basic principles for refugee rights and then to determine obligations that States are prepared to accept. How State interests and refugee rights are to be balanced lie at the centre of the debate over reform of the international refugee regime. The scope and the nature of the 1951 Refugee Convention is discussed within the overarching international legal paradigms and political contexts below.

## Refugee Law And The 1951 Convention

The 1951 Convention for the Status of Refugees is the centrepiece or at least a visible symbol of international refugee law. It is best known for its two vital contributions, the 'Convention definition' (Article 1) and the doctrine of *non-*

---

[128] Friedrich Kratochwil, 'International Law as an Approach to International Ethics: A Plea for a Jurisprudential Diagnostics' (2001)

[129] Mark Gibney, *Ethics and Refugees* (2001):

[130] Gil Loescher, *Beyond Charity: International Cooperation and the Global Refugee Crisis* (Oxford University Press 1993)

[131] James C Hathaway, *The Law of Refugee Status*, vol 104 (Oxford Univ Press 1991): 124

*refoulement* (Article 33). It is primarily concerned with the relationship between the receiving State and the asylum seeker and matters pertaining to legal status. It is thus a relatively modest enterprise - dealing only with a part of the "refugee cycle" namely the arrival of the refugee in the host or country of asylum. It does not address root causes of the refugee phenomenon or even the country of origin but rather the symptoms within its ambit- it is not pro-active or preventive of displacement. Law is disengaged with issues beyond the determination of refugee status, such as 'durable solutions'. It has mostly nothing to say about refugee camps, safe third countries or internally displaced persons. Since it does not deal with the causes of migration it cannot relate to linkages between development and forced migration[132]. There are serious omissions in relation to women, children and other categories of refugees. As a result, there are 'more gaps than structure' in international refugee law [133].

The vital concepts of 'asylum' and 'protection' are not defined in the Convention [134]. Kennedy points out that texts from the early periods 'delimit no coherent doctrinal notion of asylum, let alone one of a particularly national discretionary or political form'[135]. More recent efforts to codify an institution of asylum (the right of the State to grant asylum and for the individual to receive asylum being considered separate) have been unsuccessful. Instead, the asylum doctrine has emerged from a negative right or *non-refoulement*. For refugee legal concepts, including the components of the refugee definition, one has to turn to the non-binding UNHCR handbook [136] or to other parts of international law. The UNHCR (United Nations High Commissioner for Refugees) has played a noticeable role in facilitating the development of a more comprehensive international refugee law[137]. The UNHCR statute identifies its role as including the search for permanent solutions for the problem of refugees by assisting Governments. Yet the UNHCR itself a State creation and has had mixed success in getting States to live up to their commitments.

---

[132] Richard Black, *Refugees, Environment and Development* (Longman 1998)
[133] Arthur C Helton, *The Price of Indifference: Refugees and Humanitarian Action in the New Century* (Oxford University Press on Demand 2002)
[134] Antonio Fortin, 'The Meaning of 'Protection'in the Refugee Definition' (2000) 12 International Journal of Refugee Law 548
[135] David Kennedy, 'International Refugee Protection' (1986) 8 Human Rights Quarterly 1: 42
[136] United Nations High Commissioner for Refugees, *Handbook on Procedures and Criteria for Determining Refugee Status* (1992):
[137] Corinne Lewis, 'Unhcr's Contribution to the Development of International Refugee Law: Its Foundations and Evolution' (2005) 17 International Journal of Refugee Law 67

The *travaux* or drafting documents of the 1951 Convention show that it is a historically contingent and Eurocentric document[138]. Its main objective was "to create secure conditions such as would facilitate the sharing of the European refugee burden" [139]. The Convention definition was limited by its application to persons displaced "[a]s a result of events occurring before 1 January 1951". It also refers to European refugee agreements undertaken during the interim period between World War I and World War II and the Constitution of the International Refugee Organization. The European refugee paradigm was given global applicability through the 1967 Protocol to the 1951 Convention which merely removed the geographical and temporal restricts to make it globally applicable for all contexts. However, the 1967 Protocol missed a historic opportunity to broaden the substantive content, orientation or scope of the 1951 Convention. Instead its ideological thrust favoured the strategic dimension to induce flight toward 'pro-Western political values'[140] and 'the subtler Eurocentric Cold War biases of the Convention proved harder to eliminate' [141]. Even the end of the cold war and the advance of globalisation did not prompt a fundamental rethink of the foundations of European concepts of refugee law[142].

The 1951 Convention does not begin by speaking of the rights of refugees but of the latter's duties owed to the host State (Article 2). However, a closer look at the document yields an array of civil and political rights from the significant principles of non-discrimination (Article 3), recognition of personal status (article 12), rights to property (Articles 14 and 15), to freedom of movement and access to courts (Article 16). There is also a range of socio-economic rights which deal with employment, rationing, education and labour rights. With respect of some of these rights (for example primary education) the refugee is on par with nationals but with respect to other rights (such as higher education), refugees are merely to be given rights as 'aliens' or non-nationals. There are specific provisions relating to administrative assistance (article 25), issue of identity papers and travel documents (article 27 and 28) and significantly exemption from penalties in respect of illegal entry or presence (article 31). However, it is the principle of *non-refoulement* as both a provision in

---

[138] Paul Weis, 'The Refugee Convention, 1951: The Travaux Preparatoires Analysed, with a Commentary by Dr Paul Weis' (1995) The Research Centre for International Law, University of Cambridge
[139] Hathaway, *The Law of Refugee Status:* 9
[140] Loescher, *Beyond Charity: International Cooperation and the Global Refugee Crisis:* 55
[141] Ahilan T Arulanantham, 'Restructured Safe Havens: A Proposal for Reform of the Refugee Protection System' (2000) 22 Human Rights Quarterly 1: 5
[142] Anthony H Richmond, 'Globalization: Implications for Immigrants and Refugees' (2002) 25 Ethnic and Racial Studies 707

Article 33 of the Convention and as a principle of customary international law (applicable even if States have not signed the Convention) which drives the obligations of States towards refugees. Despite debates surrounding the nature and scope of *non-refoulement* States at least formally acknowledge the notion of limits on their discretion.

Disenchantment with the 1951 Convention from both refugee rights advocates and States demonstrates the polarity of expectations. It has been matched by anxiety that reopening of the treaty would unravel even the veneer of consensus. As a result, the UNHCR has initiated a "Convention Plus" consultative process to hold on to the minimalist 1951 Convention and its 1967 Protocol while seeking further special agreements with States, particularly on resettlement, targeting of development assistance and management of irregular secondary flows[143]. These initiatives take place even as States adopt more restrictive asylum policies negating the spirit of the 1951 Convention. European Union countries have not only adopted the least-common-denominator refugee definition but embraced coordinated measures through "soft" laws designed to deter displaced persons from exercising their right to seek asylum- for example the 1990 Dublin Convention. Following the entry into force of the Treaty of Amsterdam, Asylum and immigration issues, have now moved from the 'third' to the 'first' pillar of the EU- that is, Europe wide legal instruments are being adopted in this area which was earlier seen as matters for exclusive national jurisdiction. A fuller exploration of European Asylum laws is beyond the scope of this chapter but it suffices to say that though the EU constantly alludes to the 1951 Convention, it proceeds to violate the spirit of the treaty by legislating in areas the Convention is either ambiguous or silent.

## Importance Of The Convention Definition Of A Refugee

States see the primary role of the 1951 Convention as a status-granting mechanism. Chimni argues that this has to do with the unevenness of international refugee law itself which seems to be preoccupied with questions of definition at the expense of other related areas[144]. These include the distinction between refugees and voluntary migrants, the rights of refugees, legal aspects of the solution of voluntary repatriation, and the law of State responsibility (holding the State accountable for violation of its obligations towards refugees). A fundamental question is whether the Convention, which is selective in its choice of issues, can offer a credible

---

[143] Erika Feller, Volker Türk and Frances Nicholson, *Refugee Protection in International Law: Unhcr's Global Consultations on International Protection* (Cambridge University Press 2003)
[144] Bhupinder Singh Chimni, *International Refugee Law: A Reader* (SAGE Publications Pvt. Limited 2000): xv

definition when it is reluctant to engage with the totality of the refugee experience. Kourula[145] argues that the refugee concept can be expanded only through a reality check arising out of interplay of international responses from conflict resolution to coordination in humanitarian efforts. In contrast to popular conceptions of "refugee" arising out of the forced migration, law strives to monopolise and stamp its authority on the field of refugee definition. Rather than "declare" or confirm existing notions of refugeehood, it attempts - through its restrictive constructions - to re- constitute the refugee.

The significance of a legal definition is obvious. It is not an academic formula, but one employed by the State and which determines the legal status and entitlements of asylum seekers. Most States which have ratified the 1951 Convention use the Convention definition. Thus, a 'Convention refugee' is a refugee whose circumstances fit the criteria laid out by the Convention. Refugees falling outside the net, even though it is recognised by others are 'non-Convention refugees'. Their legal status falls within the domain of discretion or the 'humanitarian' sphere and they are not covered by the State obligations assumed under the 1951 Convention. The 'non-convention' refugees are also called *de facto* refugees as contrasted with *de jure* (legally recognised) refugees. These are not neat categories with the result that a high percentage of the displaced people do not have their rights recognised and live in a form of legal limbo. This is largely because forced migrants (protected by international law) and voluntary migrants (who are not) are often genuinely or deliberately confused to the detriment of the refugee[146].

The Convention refugee definition is not innocent. It was configured primarily as a means of identifying those to be selected for asylum but equally has operated as a means for exclusion. Refugees continue to flee for a variety of complex reasons (see chapter 4) but the law offering asylum is willing to consider only five distinct factors of expulsion pertaining to persecution– race, religion, nationality, membership in a particular social group or political opinion. Many common reasons for flight have been shunted into the 'humanitarian' bracket, outside legally justifiable reasons for refugee status [147]. As Black and Koser observe, States also have come to view the refugee determination process with considerable suspicion.

---

[145] Pirkko Kourula, *Broadening the Edges: Refugee Definition and International Protection Revisited*, vol 1 (Martinus Nijhoff Publishers 1997)

[146] Aristide R Zolberg, Astri Suhrke and Sergio Aguayo, *Escape from Violence: Conflict and the Refugee Crisis in the Developing World* (Oxford University Press on Demand 1992)

[147] Roger Zetter, 'Labelling Refugees: Forming and Transforming a Bureaucratic Identity' (1991) 4 Journal of refugee studies 39: 48

Refugee status is too often seen by policy makers as something 'exploited' by individual migrants to circumvent normal immigration rules (and one which provides much greater security and social welfare benefits), rather than an important safety net of protection for those genuinely suffering persecution[148].

One feature of the 1951 Convention is the choice of an 'abstract' approach of legal reasoning over a categorical identification of the conditions which would automatically create a refugee. This has not only signified the triumph of law over other understandings of the refugee but has fostered unfortunate characterisations of 'genuine' and 'bogus'. Strictly speaking there is no such demarcation - rather the appropriate legal query is whether the asylum applicant is covered under the Convention or not. It is precisely because law is presented as an incomprehensible, abstract or complex set of criteria to the general public that it often appears inaccessible. The legalism of the definition is problematic for both decision makers in the refugee determination process and refugees. Officials, absorbed in technical formalism, find it difficult to comprehend the true nature of the refugee experience through the personal and tragic consequences of global forced migration [149]. On the other hand, the refugee - who is expected to know and articulate refugee law - is more likely to possess a 'refugee consciousness' rather than an identity or mentality, let alone a conscious legal personality [150].

Zetter[151] shows how stereotyped identities are translated into bureaucratically assumed needs. Stressing the dynamic nature of refugee identities, Zetter is critical of the non-participatory nature and powerlessness of refugees in these processes. The stereotypical view of the refugee as dependent and parasitic on host communities runs counter to the resilience and experience of refugees the world over [152]. Rather than a single linear status, there is often an ambiguity/shifting of the refugee labels where the same person could be 'a *refugee* to one agency and an *economic migrant* to another'[153]. Law fails to recognise that refugee experiences,

---

[148] Richard Black and Khalid Koser, *The End of the Refugee Cycle?: Refugee Repatriation and Reconstruction*, vol 4 (Berghahn Books 1999): 4

[149] Alastair Ager, 'Perspectives on the Refugee Experience' (1999) Refugees: Perspectives on the Experience of Forced Migration 1: 2

[150] Tasoulla Hadjiyanni, *The Making of a Refugee: Children Adopting Refugee Identity in Cyprus* (Greenwood Publishing Group 2002): 2

[151] Zetter, 'Labelling Refugees: Forming and Transforming a Bureaucratic Identity'

[152] B Lacey Andrews, *When Is a Refugee Not a Refugee?: Flexible Social Categories and Host/Refugee Relations in Guinea* (United nations High commissioner for refugees (UNHCR) 2003) Shelly Dick, *Liberians in Ghana: Living without Humanitarian Assistance* (United nations High commissioner for refugees (UNHCR) 2002)

[153] Hadjiyanni, *The Making of a Refugee: Children Adopting Refugee Identity in Cyprus:*

practices and engagements arise out of dynamic negotiations, contestations and choices where the refugee is an active player[154]. Legal definitions do not deal with spatial factors or distances, the flight or transits, camps or urban refugees. In its attempts to give refugee a definite and limiting character, legal definitions disapproves of the idea of distinctiveness or a refusal to be persecuted. Rather than square up to the complexity of today's flight patterns and dynamics, refugee law seeks to deny its relevance.

The definition limitations in Article 1 of the 1951 Convention are accompanied by expulsion of those who fall out of the Convention (Article 1D) and those who are excluded from it (Article 1F). Article 1D stipulates that "this Convention shall not apply to persons who are at present receiving from organs or agencies of the United Nations other than the United Nations High Commissioner for Refugees protection or assistance". This operates to exclude Palestinian refugees from the purview of the 1951 Convention, despite the estimated five million Palestinians being the largest and longest existing refugee population[155]. Though the Convention should reapply 'when such protection or assistance has ceased for any reason' as per Article 1D[156], Palestinian refugees are still excluded- this despite the absence of a 'protection' agency (for example the UNHCR). The United Nations Relief and Works Agency for Palestinian Refugees in the Near East (UNWRA) provides humanitarian support but not 'protection' which was to be offered by the Nations Conciliation Commission on Palestine (UNCCP) until its collapse in the mid-1950s.Palestinian refugees in UNWRA camps are applied the UNWRA definition, though in some Western countries they could be entitled to the general definition.

## The Definition Under The 1951 Convention

A Refugee is recognised as such by the 1951 Convention only if he or she is able to negotiate a series of legal obstacles. First, the asylum claimant should be outside the country of persecution, be able to establish 'a well-founded fear of persecution' which must be linked to one of the five enumerated five grounds, and further show that the State of origin or the persecuting State is 'unable to or unwilling' to provide persecution. Thus, Article 1 considers a refugee to be one, who

---

4
[154] Nadje Al-Ali and Khalid Koser, *New Approaches to Migration?: Transnational Communities and the Transformation of Home* (Routledge 2003)
[155] Siraj Sait, 'International Refugee Law: Excluding the Palestinians' (2002) Law After Ground Zero 11
[156] Alex Takkenberg, *The Status of Palestinian Refugees in International Law* (Oxford University Press on Demand 1998)

owing to a well-founded fear of being persecuted for reasons of race, religion, nationality, membership in a particular social group, or political opinion, is outside the country of his nationality, and is unable to or, owing to such fear, is unwilling to avail himself of the protection of that country.

This definition is problematic on several fronts. First, the orientation on civil and political rights orientation appears to exclude socio-economic deprivations which could cause flight. Second, by insisting on an individualist determination of refugee status, it cannot deal with group situations and mass exodus. In effect, the refugee determination process yields results based on pre-selection of those to be granted access to the asylum system.

Definitions which emerged in the aftermath of the First World War were linked to the structures of the modern nation state and the nation building process[157]. The post-war individual identification of the refugee was in contrast to the largely collective recognition of refugees and other transitional arrangements earlier. As Hathaway points out, the conceptualisation of the refugee moved from the purely juridical (whether the refugee was legally protected in his or her country of origin) to the social (based on the factual situation) before the individualist perspectives emerged[158]. Opportunities to revisit the Convention definition through the 1967 protocol or the 1977 Draft Declaration on Territorial Asylum were missed.

The first requirement of the 1951 definition is 'alienage' - that the refugee must outside the State of origin. This must be seen in the context of the absence of a refugee visa and the pre-entry controls that refugee hosting states place on displaced persons. These have implications for Stateless persons, those with dual or multiple nationality, and refugees *sur place* (those who become refugees as a result of events after their migration). It is 'alienage', however, that effectively excludes internally displaced persons (IDPs) from the purview of the 1951 Convention [159], though others argue that it should not be a necessary condition for establishing refugee status [160]. Whether IDPs would be better off under the 1951 Convention which is weak but at least widely accepted or whether a separate more responsive regime is preferable continues to be debated. It is ironic that the UN Guiding Principles on Internal Displacement of 1998 provide a much broader definition of an Internally displaced person than is available for the internationally displaced person, the refugee. The Guidelines describe the IDP as

---

[157] Peter Taylor, *States of Terror : Democracy and Political Violence* (BBC Books 1993)
[158] Hathaway, *The Law of Refugee Status:* 2
[159] Ibid 29
[160] Andrew E Shacknove, 'Who Is a Refugee?' (1985) 95 Ethics 274

*persons or groups of persons forced or obliged to flee or to leave their homes, in particular to avoid the effects of armed conflict, situations of generalized violence, violations of human rights or natural or human-made disasters, and who have not crossed an internationally recognized State border.*

One of the main reasons for IDPs having been omitted from the 1951 Convention is that, in view of the concepts of sovereignty and territorial integrity, international law considers the State of origin to have primary responsibility regarding the displaced, rather than the international community [161]. This is a specious deference to the State simply because it is likely that that the State of origin could well be the persecutor or the tolerator of persecution. However, it is a manifestation of the limits of international law itself and a concern about the resources which characterises the IDP as a 'failed' refugee because the IDP is unable to cross international borders and is therefore entitled only to limited recognition and protection. What the Convention definition does is to privilege a narrow class of asylum seekers as refugees just as it expels a majority from its domain. It has also been pointed out that by excluding not only IDPs but a whole range of refugees, there is an inequity of outcomes- with a small range of refugee attaining protection, while the majority are left protectionless.

Asylum seekers (a term not defined in the Convention) able to establish a 'well-founded fear of persecution' must further establish that the persecution arose out of one of the five Convention grounds - race, religion, nationality, membership in a particular social group or political opinion. Failure to do so would put them outside the Convention protection. Each one of these undefined concepts has been subject to debate as to the nature and scope. The most flexible of the concepts has been 'membership of a particular social group' through which gender violence and persecution based on sexual orientation have been addressed though its results have been uneven and unpredictable [162]. The 'persecution' requirement in the Convention definition immediately excludes a large number of forced migrants fleeing man made or natural disasters. As law would have it, development-based refugees, environmental refugees or those fleeing natural disasters, general forced conscription or a war situation or civil war are not covered if they cannot show they are being targeted. Those fleeing generalized violence, systematic human rights

---

[161] Guy S Goodwin-Gill, Jane Mcadam and Jane Mcadam, *The Refugee in International Law*, vol 12 (Clarendon Press Oxford 1996): 264

[162] Derek Mcghee, 'Persecution and Social Group Status: Homosexual Refugees in the 1990s' (2001) 14 Journal of Refugee Studies 20 Karen Musalo and Stephen Knight, 'Steps Forward and Steps Back: Uneven Progress in the Law of Social Group and Gender-Based Claims in the United States' (2001) 13 Int'l J Refugee L 51

violations or foreign occupation do not have the right to seek asylum under a strict interpretation of the Convention definition.

Literature on refugee definition has focused on its most obvious failing – lack of appreciation of gender based or gender motivated violence [163]. The Convention does not explicitly recognize gender persecution as one of its grounds. A common argument is that the Convention must be amended to add a sixth ground, but it is through "soft law" (emerging principles which are not fully binding on States) approaches and innovative interpretations that refugee law attempts to be more gender neutral. Gaps relating to women refugees lie not only in the substantive laws but in the general lack of gender sensitivity in refugee determination procedures and practice. However, rather than a male centred omission of gender violence, exclusion of various forms of persecution are related to the dichotomy of public-private in international law. Firs, the assumption is that persecution in the private sphere wrought by private actors (as contrasted by the State or official realm) cannot be dealt with as effectively is because of the 'attributability' problem- States cannot be held directly responsible for the forced migration. Within the State centred international law, holding the State accountable for non-State actions is difficult. Second, various forms of gender persecution are not recognized because of the dominance of the civil and political rights conceptions of international law. Finally, the State shows a general deference to the institution of the family and societal practices even though the family and society are often sites of power relations and causes of gender rights violations. As Sullivan argues, however, these are largely political choices and boundaries of law which can and are being challenged [164].

One of the features of the refugee definition is its silence on the terms in its conditions for refugeehood. For example, 'asylum' is not defined and is left to States 'to interpret the terms of the Convention Protocol and to set up their own national procedures, subject to various instruments' [165]. This is another example of the State-centeredness of international refugee law. As discussed in the previous chapter, this is overcome to some degree by reliance on international human rights treaties and there have been some innovative approaches within State processes that have favoured the refugee. The main part of the definition which requires a 'well-founded fear of persecution' requires an evaluation of subjective fear through an externally verifiable objective test. What threshold of risk is required - imminent,

---

[163] Jacqueline Greatbatch, 'The Gender Difference: Feminist Critiques of Refugee Discourse' (1989) 1 International Journal of Refugee Law 518

[164] Donna Sullivan, 'The Public/Private Distinction in International Human Rights Law' (1995) Women's rights, human rights: International feminist perspectives 126

[165] Hélène Lambert, *Seeking Asylum: Comparative Law and Practice in Selected European Countries*, vol 37 (Martinus Nijhoff 1995): 3

reasonable or likely - has been adopted variously by different States. This is particularly problematic since 'persecution', which covers both physical and psychological harm, has not been spelt out. Contemporary debates have revolved around the source of risk particularly from non-State actors: the distinction between prosecution and persecution particularly laws of general application and threats without punitive intent such as injurious cultural practices, notably female genital mutilation. The rights of child refugees are an example where the silence of the 1951 Convention is sought to be overcome by reliance on other parts of international law, for example the 1989 Convention on the Rights of the Child as well as national law or policy [166].

## Alternatives To The 1951 Refugee Definition

The 1951 definition prevails as a tenuous and continuing compromise between States which consider it too broad and refugee advocates who argue the opposite. However, in several regions there have long been broader definitions [167]. For example, the 1969 Convention Governing the Specific Aspects of Refugee Problems in Africa adds that

> 'the term 'refugee' shall also apply to every person who, owing to external aggression, occupation, foreign domination or events seriously disturbing public order in either part or the whole of his country of origin or nationality, is compelled to leave his place of habitual residence in order to seek refuge in another place outside his country his country of origin or nationality'.

The 1984 Cartagena Declaration which is not binding but influential in Latin American countries, considers refugees to include:

> 'persons who have fled their country because their lives, safety or freedom have been threatened by generalised violence, foreign aggression, internal conflicts, massive violation of human rights of other circumstances which have seriously disturbed public order" (part III, para, 3).

In Europe, where there is no regional refugee treaty, there is a dual policy of recognising the 1951 Convention while developing strategies that largely violate its spirit [168]. This takes place in several ways. First, there is an intensification of refugee

---

[166] Cynthia Price Cohen, 'United Nations Convention on the Rights of the Child: Implications for Change in the Care and Protection of Refugee Children, The' (1991) 3 Int'l J Refugee L 675

[167] Richard Plender, 'Basic Documents on International Migration Law' (1997)

containment policies with the aim of ensuring that refugees to not reach the continent and that fewer access the Convention protection net. Second, the adoption of a harmonised approach to the refugee definition since at least 1996 has lowered standards of refugee recognition. Third, despite moves towards a common European asylum system, as developed through the burden-sharing 1990 Dublin Convention, still contains highly restrictive approaches as well as inconsistencies, for example on recognising persecution from non-State actors. Robust national court battles are being fought over the meaning of the refugee and the implications of refugee rights under the 1951 Convention and other human rights instruments.

## The Internationality Of Refugee Law

A major criticism of international refugee law is that it does not deal with the causes of migration, the "refugee cycle" or the 'durable' solutions. Rather than engage the totality of the refugee experience, it identifies the phase that concerns the host State. International refugee law shows a disregard not only for the factors of globalisation and newer forms of conflict [169], but is disconnected from general theories of migration which too often do not consider the impact of legal agendas [170]. International law been subject to critiques, for example from the feminists on the male constructions of refugees and gender deprecating applications [171]. It has also been seen as partial. Crisp argues refugee producing States cannot hide behind arguments of sovereignty and non-intervention protocols and that the international community must adopt more comprehensive measures to deal with refugee protection[172]. However, how and when the international community can and must intervene in the name of refugees is a matter of debate.

The key problem lies in lack of a methodology for inclusivity within the international legal discourse. Despite the need for an interdisciplinary and cross-cultural approach to migration studies [173], "there is an absence of a tradition in the literature on refugee law debating issues from the wider social science perspective" [174].

---

[168] Danièle Joly, *Haven or Hell?: Asylum Policies and Refugees in Europe* (Macmillan Press 1996)

[169] Richmond, 'Globalization: Implications for Immigrants and Refugees'

[170] Douglas S Massey and others, 'Theories of International Migration: A Review and Appraisal' (1993) Population and development review 431

[171] Hilary Charlesworth and Christine Mary Chinkin, *The Boundaries of International Law: A Feminist Analysis* (Manchester University Press 2000)

[172] Jeff Crisp, *A New Asylum Paradigm?: Globalization, Migration and the Uncertain Future of the International Refugee Regime* (United nations High commissioner for refugees (UNHCR) 2003)

[173] Anthony H Richmond, 'Migration Theory: Talking across Disciplines' (2001) 14 Journal of Refugee Studies 331

Though principles governing relations between States in peace and war have existed in various forms in numerous ancient and more contemporary formulations, there is little dispute that contemporary international law has a marked Christian European origin traceable at least to the 1648 Peace of Westphalia [175]. International refugee law emerging uncritically from European refugee law (see the 1951 Convention below) has intrinsic limitations in its claim for universal protection for refugees from all parts of the world (see chapter 2). The 1951 Convention has been ratified by many States but their compliance with its provisions has generally been selective and inconsistent. The assertion that the corpus of rules built around the 1951 Convention constitutes a 'universal' or 'international' refugee law has been challenged, though the dominant western refugee discourse generally ignores it [176].

The prevailing 'Law of Nations' is said to have emerged from the principles of reason, justice and the laws of practice of 'civilised' nations [177]. This imprint of international law has long been seen as the preserve of an ideologically superior society of modern nation States. The International Court of Justice, in its Charter identifying the sources of international law, still listens only to general principles of law recognised by 'civilised nations' (Article 38), even though the idea of 'civilised' is not formally or widely used today. For the refugee, this dichotomy of 'civilised-uncivilised' States has been problematic. Some have benefited during the ideological one-upmanship, for example during the cold war, but most others have been tainted by association with the 'uncivilised' State. Though it is those very States who often persecute or repudiate them. Here, the refugee in international law emerges as the classic 'other' from the 'other'.

Davies notes that 'the 'East' and 'West' have taken up very different positions in relation to refugees [178]. This explains, she claims, why only five Asian countries have ratified the 1951 Convention while 15 others have refused to do so. African countries have often complained that international refugee law does not recognize their distinctive refugee experiences and patterns which have been 'severely affected by the colonial experience which, in turn, influenced economic, socio-cultural, political, and demographic development' [179]. As a result, regional refugee frameworks in

---

[174] Chimni, *International Refugee Law: A Reader*: xv
[175] Peter Malanczuk, *Akehurst's Modern Introduction to International Law* (Routledge 2002): 9
[176] Bhupinder S Chimni, 'The Geopolitics of Refugee Studies: A View from the South' (1998) 11 Journal of Refugee Studies 350; Susan Musarrat Akram, 'Orientalism Revisited in Asylum and Refugee Claims' (2000) 12 International Journal of Refugee Law 7
[177] James L Brierley, 'The Law of Nations' (1963) Oxford etc 62: 41
[178] Sara Davies, ''Truly'international Refugee Law? Or yet Another East/West Divide?' (2002) 21 Social Alternatives 37

Africa and Latin America (see below) have moved away from the limitations of the 1951 Conventions, and the UNHCR with its 68-member Executive Committee (including States who are not signatories to the 1951 Convention) strives to seek innovative approaches to refugee protection.

## The Refugee In International Law

The refugee is one of the very few categories or subscribers of State law without an input into its making. Here law operates despite the expectation that a refugee is supposed to know what the international law or national law –really the State- expects of the refugee. In the State's appropriation of refugee law, argues Tuitt, there is an 'irreparable conflict between international refugee law and the refugee' [180]. Cholewinski discusses how throughout history aliens have always been treated differently from citizens. Traditional constructions of aliens have their roots 'deep in primitive suspicions and fears of the outsider', he observes [181]. Shah, who researches the use of law to target African and Asian refugee groups in the UK, argues that despite the centrality of race in response to refugee movements, this dimension is understudied and understated [182]. Though there are emerging standards relating to treatment of migrants, they have in general have been accorded inferior status in society and at the work place [183].

After World War II, international law expanded into newer fields such as human rights and refugee law. This has been accompanied by the recognition of new 'subjects' – individuals such as refugees [184]. Recognition of refugees as 'actors' rather than passive beneficiaries of State discretion has been difficult. As Loescher notes: 'Governments have traditionally sought to preserve their territorial sovereignty by controlling their borders. In no area do they more jealously guard their sovereignty than in immigration affairs' [185]. However, refugees bereft of the luxury of the 'refugee visa' and facing increasing pre-entry control efforts from

---

[179] Ali A Mazrui, 'The African State as a Political Refugee: Institutional Collapse And' (1995) Human Displacement, Int'l J Refugee L, Summer 21; Johnathan Bascom, 'The New Nomads' (1995) The migration experience in Africa 197

[180] Patricia Tuitt, *False Images: Law's Construction of the Refugee* (Pluto Pr 1996): 5

[181] Ryszard Ignacy Cholewinski, *Migrant Workers in International Human Rights Law: Their Protection in Countries of Employment* (Oxford University Press 1997): 40

[182] Prakash Shah, *Refugees, Race and the Legal Concept of Asylum in Britain* (Routledge 2000): 5

[183] Stephen Castles and Godula Kosack, *Immigrant Workers and Class Structure in Western Europe* (Oxford University Press London 1973)

[184] Malanczuk, *Akehurst's Modern Introduction to International Law:* 1

[185] Loescher, *Beyond Charity: International Cooperation and the Global Refugee Crisis:* 129

Western States have been compelled to bypass State refugee-processing channels and are thus seen as challenging State authority. It is here that international law, disinterested in refugee flight patterns, yields to the State which uses its national laws to criminalise the refugee. Demuth notes that illegality is an artificial product, the outcome of negative laws that selectively define and prohibit so that an increasing number of undocumented migrants become illegal by default as doors to 'legal' entry are shut [186].

There is no general right to freedom of movement across borders for non-nationals. A key attribute of sovereignty is, and always has been, the right to grant or refuse aliens access to one's territory [187]. There are arguments to the effect that closed borders are a departure from historical norms and the law should recognize at least some elements of freedom of movement [188]. However, national immigration laws are among the most prolific legislative activity in the past decade in a large number of countries. Neuman points out that contrary to the myth of open borders in the United States, immigration controls have a long history [189]. The 1948 Universal Declaration of Human Rights, the pioneering human rights document which is influential though not binding, recognises the right to asylum. Article 14 declares that 'Everyone has the right to seek and to enjoy in other countries asylum from persecution'. A closer reading shows that it does not create a corresponding duty for States to grant asylum, though other parts of international law - particularly *non-refoulement* emphasise the obligation that the State must consider asylum requests [190].

From the point of view of legal drama, the tussle between the State and the refugee is fascinating but often has tragic consequences for the latter. In a cat-and-mouse game of moves and counter moves, the State seeks to quell what it calls 'asylum shopping' while the refugee seeks escape from the cycle of being a 'refugee in orbit' [191]. Before this century, refugees were generally 'regarded as assets rather

---

[186] Andreas Demuth, 'Some Conceptual Thoughts on Migration Research' (2000) Theoretical and Methodological Issues in Migration Research: Interdisciplinary, intergenerational and international perspectives, Ashgath Publishers: Aldershot 21: 42

[187] N Mole, 'Immigration and Freedom of Movement' in D and Joseph Harris, S (ed), The International Covenant on Civil and Political Rights and United Kingdom Law (Clarendon Press 1995): 297

[188] Satvinder S Juss, 'Free Movement and the World Order' (2004) 16 International Journal of Refugee Law 289

[189] Gerald L Neuman, *Strangers to the Constitution: Immigrants, Borders, and Fundamental Law* (Princeton University Press 2010): 19

[190] Kennedy, 'International Refugee Protection' 57

[191] Nicholas Van Hear, *New Diasporas: The Mass Exodus, Dispersal and Regrouping of Migrant Communities* (London, UCL Press 1998): 59

than liabilities; countries granted refuge to people of geopolitical, religious, or ideological views similar to their own; and rulers viewed control over large populations, along with natural resources and territory itself, as an index of power and national greatness' [192]. However, the "new" refugees who take the initiative to secure safety in the West incur the wrath of the State which fear a loss of control.

National asylum laws often unleash their exclusionary powers or discriminate against asylum seekers supposedly because of how they enter, despite the 1951 Refugee Convention (article 31) prohibiting penalisation due to manner of entry. This relates to characterizing asylum seekers on where they come from. Governments of Western States in particular often perceive their societies as vulnerable to the fallout from an increasingly brutal and chaotic world and respond with draconian legislation [193]. Numbers or perceptions of mass influx are certainly a factor, but it is the variability of the manner of entry of forced migrants that beguiles the State which either deliberately promotes the idea of uncontrollable 'bogus' asylum claimants or tolerates the spread of such public imagining. The relationship between media representations of the refugee, public anxiety, political brinkmanship and the push towards hostile refugee law has been well established [194].

Backers [195] argues that Western governments who attempt 'to construct a one-dimensional paradigm that conflates the trafficking and smuggling of refugees and treat all such activity as purely criminal' often miss the complexity, variety and contexts of refugee flight arrangements made. Koser [196] explains the dilemma:

On the one hand, advocates are concerned that successfully stamping out smuggling would deprive many people of the possibility of seeking asylum in the industrialized nations, but on the other hand they can hardly be seen to support a system that exploits asylum seekers. At least partly as a result of this quandary, asylum advocates – including the United Nations High Commissioner for Refugees – have been surprisingly reticent in the human smuggling debate, and legislation by states to stop smuggling has advanced more or less unchallenged, despite its implications for asylum.

---

[192] Loescher, *Beyond Charity: International Cooperation and the Global Refugee Crisis*: 32

[193] James C Hathaway and Colin J Harvey, 'Framing Refugee Protection in the New World Disorder' (2001) 22 Immigr & Nat'lity L Rev 191

[194] Philip Marfleet, *Refugees in a Global Era* (Palgrave Macmillan Basingstoke 2006)

[195] Sharone Backers, 'Risking It All: The Implications of Refugee Smuggling' (2001) 43 Race & class 75

[196] Khalid Koser, 'Reconciling Control and Compassion? Human Smuggling and the Right to Asylum', E. Newman and J. Van Selm' (2003) Refugees and Forced Displacement: International Security, Human Vulnerability 181: 181

While every claimant for asylum is presumed to be entitled to the benefit of the Convention pending refugee determination [197], dominant media characterisations feed public images that these are largely "economic migrants" arriving under false pretences. National asylum laws have been continuously tightened in response to national security considerations as well as the perception that they obstruct efficient enforcement of a restrictive immigration policy [198]. For Tuitt, refugee law is designed "not to offer a solution to refugee problems, but to control those migration flows which cannot be curtailed by the simple transference between economic and involuntary migration' [199]. The law is not a level playing field for the refugee, who not only finds the law 'alien' and inscrutable but also expensive and time consuming. There is generally little legal aid and support for the refugees- often the most marginalised of the vulnerable- to access justice and human rights conceived for the nationals.

---

[197] J Hathaway and A Neve, 'Making International Law Relevant Again: A Proposal for Collectivized Solution-Orientated Protection' (1997) 10 Harv Hum Rts J 115: 158

[198] Niraj Nathwani, 'The Purpose of Asylum' (2000) 12 International Journal of Refugee Law 354

[199] Tuitt, *False Images: Law's Construction of the Refugee*: 5

## Conclusion

International refugee law offers some protection standards for States to follow, or at least consider. However, the poverty of international refugee law arises from the cumulative debilitating effect of the inferior personhood of the refugee as well as the State-centeredness of international law. The projection of law by the State as the final non-negotiable ruling is misconceived and thankfully a fiction. Refugees, on the other hand, recognise the pluralism, malleability and opportunities that law offers, however limited it may seem at first. Law's apparent resistance to interdisciplinary and cross-cultural dialogue as well as its general inaccessibility to refugees renders law capable of manipulation by the State. However, the law generating process itself is not sterile but rather offers several points of entry and opportunity for refugee activists. The role, character and manifestations of law – and its pluralism- are regularly debated within academic fields but the law itself seeks exclusivity and insularity. As Harvey [200] notes, there are continuing disputes over the foundation, purposes and functions of refugee law. In this context, one must ask why certain voices dominate refugee law and why the 'Statist paradigm' prevails and how refugee law can evolve into an innovative refugee responsive system, accessible to all.

The monopolising effect of law is evident in the definition debate. The question is not whether a State constituted Refugee Convention is legal- it is. The query is whether it is legitimate, relevant and credible and whether it works. The Convention may be half a century old with Eurocentric origins, but it can either be dismissed as irrelevant or viewed, for lack of alternatives, as a 'living document' capable of evolving and of innovative interpretations beyond original intent. Talk of wholesale substitution of the 1951 Convention or the basic premises of international law is either wishful thinking or a leap into the unknown. Contending with growing State intolerance of the refugee phenomenon is more troubling. Reforms of refugee systems have, in fact, the tendency to play into the hands of States who are seeking to package their containment and refugee avoidance policies as the new international law [201]. The extent to which refugee perspectives can be incorporated into these developments remains to be seen.

Despite the endurance of the Convention definition and *non-refoulement* principle, the 1951 Convention simply did not foresee current manifestations of the

---

[200] Colin J Harvey, 'Talking About Refugee Law' (1999) 12 Journal of Refugee Studies 101
[201] Mertus, 'The State and the Post-Cold War Refugee Regime: New Models, New Questions'

refugee rights challenge. Negotiations over burden sharing and re-admission agreements, pre-entry controls, internal flight, concerns over human trafficking and criminalization of the refugee, the quality of asylum, safe third-country concepts, temporary protection approaches, and off shore refugee processing zones will continue. The very exilic basis of international refugee law has been called into question and new layers are being added piecemeal. The biggest question, however, has been the cost-effectiveness and efficiency of the 1951 Convention refugee determination process. States spend more resources on keeping out refugees and in processing their claims than in protecting them either in their country of origin or in receiving countries. Most noticeably, Convention inspired formalistic and formulaic refugee-processing approaches break down in cases of mass influx or when numbers increase or where national security considerations or political agendas reign. As the UNHCR recognizes, the "durable solutions" and the relative priority accorded to each has changed with time and must be part of multi-stakeholder and global consultations [202]. No doubt, institutional reform – be it a powerful new international refugee agency [203] or strengthening the UNHCR - will be the focus, but the dilemma is whether future developments will create a refugee law *for* refugees or simply keep it a law *about* refugees.

In a world of globalisation and conflict States seek to localise the refugee phenomenon as 'not our problem' and to render the displaced as an 'internal' (to the State of origin) and remote problem. In its treatment of asylum seekers too, the State puts its national laws above that of international standards. Partisans of international refugee law, with all its limitations, profess that law is relevant because it creates 'international' accountability. As discussed in Chapter 9, international legal discourse is only half the story- human rights responses offer an attempt to counter State monopolies of the law. Law as it stands is often an elusive framework for refugees to access and rely upon. The wheels of international refugee legal protection lack the cogs that could make it work for migrants. Legal guarantees are still largely illusory and theoretical because the tools which could make them sustainable and easily implemented are missing. Future generations of refugees, civil society, researchers, professionals and policy makers are likely to be confronted with the task of developing tools from laws which serve refugees, not merely the States.

---

[202] United Nations High Commissioner for Refugees, *The State of the World's Refugees 2006: Human Displacement in the New Millennium*
[203] Helton, *The Price of Indifference: Refugees and Humanitarian Action in the New Century*

## References

Al-Ali N and Koser K, New Approaches to Migration?: Transnational Communities and the Transformation of Home (Routledge 2003)

Andrews BL, When Is a Refugee Not a Refugee?: Flexible Social Categories and Host/Refugee Relations in Guinea (United nations High commissioner for refugees (UNHCR) 2003)

Black R, Refugees, Environment and Development (Longman 1998)

Black R and Koser K, The End of the Refugee Cycle?: Refugee Repatriation and Reconstruction, vol 4 (Berghahn Books 1999)

Castles S and Kosack G, *Immigrant Workers and Class Structure in Western Europe* (Oxford University Press London 1973)

Charlesworth H and Chinkin CM, *The Boundaries of International Law: A Feminist Analysis* (Manchester University Press 2000)

Chimni BS, *International Refugee Law: A Reader* (SAGE Publications Pvt. Limited 2000)

Cholewinski RI, Migrant Workers in International Human Rights Law: Their Protection in Countries of Employment (Oxford University Press 1997)

Crisp J, A New Asylum Paradigm?: Globalization, Migration and the Uncertain Future of the International Refugee Regime (United nations High commissioner for refugees (UNHCR) 2003)

Dick S, *Liberians in Ghana: Living without Humanitarian Assistance* (United nations High commissioner for refugees (UNHCR) 2002)

Feller E, Türk V and Nicholson F, Refugee Protection in International Law: Unhcr's Global Consultations on International Protection (Cambridge University Press 2003)

Goodwin-Gill GS, McAdam J and McAdam J, *The Refugee in International Law*, vol 12 (Clarendon Press Oxford 1996)

Hadjiyanni T, The Making of a Refugee: Children Adopting Refugee Identity in Cyprus (Greenwood Publishing Group 2002)

Hathaway JC, *The Law of Refugee Status*, vol 104 (Oxford Univ Press 1991)

Helton AC, The Price of Indifference: Refugees and Humanitarian Action in the New Century (Oxford University Press on Demand 2002)

Joly D, Haven or Hell?: Asylum Policies and Refugees in Europe (Macmillan Press 1996)

Kourula P, Broadening the Edges: Refugee Definition and International Protection Revisited, vol 1 (Martinus Nijhoff Publishers 1997)

Lambert H, Seeking Asylum: Comparative Law and Practice in Selected European Countries, vol 37 (Martinus Nijhoff 1995)

Loescher G, Beyond Charity: International Cooperation and the Global Refugee Crisis (Oxford University Press 1993)

Malanczuk P, Akehurst's Modern Introduction to International Law (Routledge 2002)

Marfleet P, *Refugees in a Global Era* (Palgrave Macmillan Basingstoke 2006)

Neuman GL, Strangers to the Constitution: Immigrants, Borders, and Fundamental Law (Princeton University Press 2010)

Shah P, Refugees, Race and the Legal Concept of Asylum in Britain (Routledge 2000)

Takkenberg A, *The Status of Palestinian Refugees in International Law* (Oxford University Press on Demand 1998)

Taylor P, States of Terror : Democracy and Political Violence (BBC Books 1993)

Tuitt P, False Images: Law's Construction of the Refugee (Pluto Pr 1996)

Zolberg AR, Suhrke A and Aguayo S, Escape from Violence: Conflict and the Refugee Crisis in the Developing World (Oxford University Press on Demand 1992)

Mole N, 'Immigration and Freedom of Movement' in Harris DaJ, S (ed), *The International Covenant on Civil and Political Rights and United Kingdom Law* (Clarendon Press 1995)

Arendt H, *The Origins of Totalitarianism* (New York: Harcourt Brace 1951)

Gibney M, Ethics and Refugees (2001)

HEAR NV, New Diasporas: The Mass Exodus, Dispersal and Regrouping of Migrant Communities (London, UCL Press 1998)

United Nations High Commissioner for Refugees, Handbook on Procedures and Criteria for Determining Refugee Status (1992)

United Nations High Commissioner for Refugees, The State of the World's Refugees 2006: Human Displacement in the New Millennium (2006)

Ager A, 'Perspectives on the Refugee Experience' (1999) Refugees: Perspectives on the Experience of Forced Migration 1

Akram SM, 'Orientalism Revisited in Asylum and Refugee Claims' (2000) 12 International Journal of Refugee Law 7

Arulanantham AT, 'Restructured Safe Havens: A Proposal for Reform of the Refugee Protection System' (2000) 22 Human Rights Quarterly 1

BACKERS S, 'Risking It All: The Implications of Refugee Smuggling' (2001) 43 Race & class 75

Barnett L, 'Global Governance and the Evolution of the International Refugee Regime' (2002) 14 International Journal of Refugee Law 238

Bascom J, 'The New Nomads' (1995) The migration experience in Africa 197

Brierley JL, 'The Law of Nations' (1963) Oxford etc 62

Chimni BS, 'The Geopolitics of Refugee Studies: A View from the South' (1998) 11 Journal of Refugee Studies 350

Cohen CP, 'United Nations Convention on the Rights of the Child: Implications for Change in the Care and Protection of Refugee Children, The' (1991) 3 Int'l J Refugee L 675

Davies S, '"Truly'international Refugee Law? Or yet Another East/West Divide?' (2002) 21 Social Alternatives 37

Demuth A, 'Some Conceptual Thoughts on Migration Research' (2000) Theoretical and Methodological Issues in Migration Research: Interdisciplinary, intergenerational and international perspectives, Ashgath Publishers: Aldershot 21

Fortin A, 'The Meaning of 'Protection'in the Refugee Definition' (2000) 12 International Journal of Refugee Law 548

Greatbatch J, 'The Gender Difference: Feminist Critiques of Refugee Discourse' (1989) 1 International Journal of Refugee Law 518

Haddad E, 'The Refugee: The Individual between Sovereigns' (2003) 17 Global Society 297

Harvey CJ, 'Talking About Refugee Law' (1999) 12 Journal of Refugee Studies 101

Hathaway J and Neve A, 'Making International Law Relevant Again: A Proposal for Collectivized Solution-Orientated Protection' (1997) 10 Harv Hum Rts J 115

Hathaway JC and Harvey CJ, 'Framing Refugee Protection in the New World Disorder' (2001) 22 Immigr & Nat'lity L Rev 191

Juss SS, 'Free Movement and the World Order' (2004) 16 International Journal of Refugee Law 289

Kennedy D, 'International Refugee Protection' (1986) 8 Human Rights Quarterly 1

Koser K, 'Reconciling Control and Compassion? Human Smuggling and the Right to Asylum', E. Newman and J. Van Selm' (2003) Refugees and Forced Displacement: International Security, Human Vulnerability 181

Kratochwil F, 'International Law as an Approach to International Ethics: A Plea for a Jurisprudential Diagnostics' (2001)

Lewis C, 'Unhcr's Contribution to the Development of International Refugee Law: Its Foundations and Evolution' (2005) 17 International Journal of Refugee Law 67

Massey DS and others, 'Theories of International Migration: A Review and Appraisal' (1993) Population and development review 431

Mazrui AA, 'The African State as a Political Refugee: Institutional Collapse And' (1995) Human Displacement, Int'l J Refugee L, Summer 21

McGhee D, 'Persecution and Social Group Status: Homosexual Refugees in the 1990s' (2001) 14 Journal of Refugee Studies 20

Mertus J, 'The State and the Post-Cold War Refugee Regime: New Models, New Questions' (1998) 10 International Journal of Refugee Law 321

Musalo K and Knight S, 'Steps Forward and Steps Back: Uneven Progress in the Law of Social Group and Gender-Based Claims in the United States' (2001) 13 Int'l J Refugee L 51

Nathwani N, 'The Purpose of Asylum' (2000) 12 International Journal of Refugee Law 354

Plender R, 'Basic Documents on International Migration Law' (1997)

Richmond AH, 'Migration Theory: Talking across Disciplines' (2001) 14 Journal of Refugee Studies 331

Richmond AH, 'Globalization: Implications for Immigrants and Refugees' (2002) 25 Ethnic and Racial Studies 707

Sait S, 'International Refugee Law: Excluding the Palestinians' (2002) Law After Ground Zero 11

Shacknove AE, 'Who Is a Refugee?' (1985) 95 Ethics 274

Sullivan D, 'The Public/Private Distinction in International Human Rights Law' (1995) Women's rights, human rights International feminist perspectives 126

Weis P, 'The Refugee Convention, 1951: The Travaux Preparatoires Analysed, with a Commentary by Dr Paul Weis' (1995) The Research Centre for International Law, University of Cambridge

Zetter R, 'Labelling Refugees: Forming and Transforming a Bureaucratic Identity' (1991) 4 Journal of refugee studies 39

# An Examination Of The Transformation Of The Border To Define States Obligations In Refugee Protection

## Stella Ngugi

*The refugee is defined in the context of the border. One cannot be considered to be a refugee until they have crossed an international border and left their country of origin. They are also expected to be physically present within the country they are seeking to claim asylum from and thus they need to cross the border of that state. Over the past few decades the refugee situation has arguably placed a socio-economical strain on states and they have taken various measures to limit the number of refugees coming into their territory. Drawing on Ayelet Shachar's argument on the concept of the shifting border I argue that states have in this regard sought to transform their borders from the physical geographical border that identifies a state on the political map to a dynamic, flexible or shifting border in order to define the parameters of where their obligations under the 1951 convention begin. Focusing on the push backs at sea in Italy and the excision of islands in Australia I argue that these methods demonstrate aggressive efforts by states to redefine their borders in order to limit or do away with their obligations under international refugee law. In this paper I will seek to show that these efforts not only undermine refugee protection and are in contravention of these states' obligations, but they are also an exercise in futility as the states responsibility to the refugee still persists.*

## Introduction

Since the beginning of the 20th Century there have been a myriad of complex conflict situations that have affected millions of lives the world over. From the first world war of 1914 to the current ongoing conflict in Syria, citizens of states have been affected by not only losing their lives or those of their loved ones but also through loss of their homes and forced displacement. When it comes to displacement of persons, the terms under which one may defined by are arguably dictated by the border. The border helps draw the distinction between whether a person is considered an internally displaced person or whether they are considered a refugee. For one to be considered a refugee they are expected to cross an international border thus in essence they should have left their country of origin. It is only at this point that reference to International Refugee Law can be made. This is because before such a crossing they are still governed by the national legislature of their country of origin as they can only be classified as internally displaced persons. Though one does not become a *de jure* refugee simply by crossing this international border, it is the fundamental prerequisite in determining one's refugee status; one cannot be a refugee in their own country. Further when one seeks to be a refugee in a certain country it has become a recognisable fact that such a person ought to be present in the country in which they are seeking asylum. In this respect again, the issue of the border comes into play as the asylum seeker cannot be considered for refugee status if he has not crossed into the country in which he is seeking asylum from.

In international refugee law, states which are a party to the 1951 Convention on the Status of Refugees have a responsibility to guarantee refugee rights by ensuring their protection against the force that is threatening their lives. With the great number of refugees that have been recorded in the past few decades, the process of guaranteeing their rights and safety has placed great socio-economic strain on host countries. Many host states have complained of the economic burden that arises from giving aid to these asylum seekers as well as the cost implications that arise from the refugee status determination processes. Additionally, many host state governments have faced serious backlash from the citizens claiming that the refugees are restricting their access to secure, sustainable jobs. Also, in the post 9/11 global reality these refugees are also perceived to either be terrorists or to be terrorist sympathizers. This continued conflict between the host government and the asylum seekers has led to a situation where the host states have decided to undertake measures to limit the numbers entering their borders.

One-way states have done this is by simply adjusting their borders. States have arguably transformed their borders from the rigid border as displayed on a political map to a dynamic border that is meant to determine when the state becomes responsible for an asylum seeker. States in some instances use this "new" border to determine if an asylum seeker has indeed crossed their border and into their territory and is thus entitled to their protection under international refugee law. Focusing on the push backs at sea in Italy and the excision of islands in Australia I argue that states have made aggressive efforts to redefine their borders in order to limit or do away with their obligations under international refugee law. In this paper I will seek to show that these efforts not only undermine refugee protection and are in contravention of these states' obligations, but they are also an exercise in futility as the states responsibility to the refugee still persists and in some cases it is extended beyond the states own territorial borders. In the first section of this essay I will show how states have shifted their borders and how the need to minimise their responsibility in international refugee law has motivated these efforts. In the second section I will demonstrate that not only do these efforts undermine refugee protection and are in contravention of the states' obligations under international refugee law, but they are an exercise in futility because their responsibility to the refugee still persists.

## The Refugee And The Border

A border can be defined simply as the line that separates two administrative areas or two countries.[204] It denotes the specific area within which a government is legally allowed to exercise administrative action over and it provides the people who live within that area with an identity and a structure of society. The border denotes political territories of states on any world map and though it is not visible to the naked eye it has a huge bearing on how both national and international affairs operate. Therefore since borders are often discussed in a political, social and cultural construct, they are primarily understood as being linked to state sovereignty and the state itself.[205] The border in essence conceptualises the idea of what is considered internal and what is considered external and consequently foreign.[206] Being tied with such crucial concepts such as state sovereignty could arguably be used to explain why the 'drawing or even dissolution of borders' may be considered as 'a demonstration of power'.[207] The border thus clearly defines each state government's

---

[204] Oxford Dictionaries, at http://www.oxforddictionaries.com/definition/english/border (April 13 2015)

[205] Veronika Magyar-Haas, "Ambivalent Concepts of the Border: Political Borders – Bodily Boundaries", Social Work and Society International Online Journal, Volume 10, Issue No. 2 (2012), at http://www.socwork.net/sws/article/view/336/673 (April 14 2015)

[206] Ibid

[207] Ibid

scope of reach and bears a great influence in how that government would relate to a foreign government whether or not it shares a border with that state. It is therefore not unimaginable that it is something that a state would jealously defend because it is closely linked with the protection of that state.

Though state borders have often been understood to be rigid and unchanging, there has been wide debate on how this is not the case as borders are changeable, usually being constructed as a result of 'political interest and decisions' made in a particular socio-historical context.[208] Therefore, as Shachar points out, the state border can easily be defined as 'moving barrier' or 'a legal construct that is not tightly fixed to territorial benchmarks'.[209] This is especially true when it comes to matters relating to immigration and in particular immigration issues relating to asylum seekers which is the focus of this paper.

As mentioned above the border is the demarcation point of inclusion and exclusion; it is what determines who is an insider and who is an outsider; thus showing why it is a crucial concept to understand in regard to immigration issues.[210] Since borders shape a state's jurisdictional frontier, the distinction between the members and non-members of the state has a direct correlation to the scope of rights and protections that can be offered to either of the two.[211] Additionally, it is the state government's prerogative to determine who is allowed into any country as the border is tied to the protection of that state. Therefore when it comes to immigration, the border denotes the point at which a state would be obliged to confer upon a person any of the rights or protections guaranteed by that state's national legislation.[212] Hence if a person has not crossed the border and entered *into* a particular state, that state is not legally obliged to confer any of its protections or rights on that person.[213] However as previously mentioned when it comes to immigration, whether or not it is related to asylum seekers, this border is not as it is displayed on the map, it is constantly shifting 'at times penetrating into the interior' and on other occasions extending beyond the ordinarily recognized territory of the state.[214]

---

[208] Magyar-Haas, Ambivalent Concepts of the Border
[209] Ayelet Shachar, "The Shifting Border of Immigration Regulation", Stanford Journal of Civic Rights and Civil Liberties, Volume 3, (2007), 167
[210] Ibid, 165
[211] Ibid, 165-6
[212] Ibid, 166
[213] Ibid
[214] Shachar, The Shifting Border, 166

The 1951 Convention on the Status of the Refugee in article 1 (A)(2) defines the refugee as:

> "*owing to well-founded fear of being persecuted for reasons of race, religion, nationality, membership of a particular social group or political opinion, is outside the country of his nationality and is unable or, owing to such fear, is unwilling to avail himself of the protection of that country; or who, not having a nationality and being outside the country of his former habitual residence as a result of such events, is unable or, owing to such fear, is unwilling to return to it*".[215]

Further, the 1969 Organisation of African Unity Convention Governing the Specific Aspects of Refugee Problems in Africa, in article 1 and 2 defines the refugee as:

> "*every person who, owing to well-founded fear of being persecuted for reasons of race, religion, nationality, membership of a particular social group or political opinion, is outside the country of his nationality and is unable or, owing to such fear, is unwilling to avail himself of the protection of that country, or who, not having a nationality and being outside the country of his former habitual residence as a result of such events, is unable or, owing to such fear, is unwilling to return to it.*
>
> *[...] owing to external aggression, occupation, foreign domination or events seriously disturbing public order in either part or the whole of his country of origin or nationality, is compelled to leave his place of habitual residence in order to seek refuge in another place outside his country of origin or nationality*".[216]

Both definitions offer slightly different parameters under which should be considered before one is determined to be a refugee. However, one thing that bears fundamental importance in both definitions is that for one to be considered as a refugee they must have crossed an internationally recognised border. Indeed, this clearly reflects a notion that borders play a vital role in shaping our understanding and discussions of refugees.[217] These definitions illustrate that for a person to claim

---

[215] Convention relating to the Status of Refugees 1951

[216] OAU Convention Governing the Specific Aspects of Refugee Problems in Africa 1969

[217] Laura Madokoro, "Borders Transformed: Sovereign Concerns, Population Movements and the Making of Territorial Frontiers in Hong Kong, 1949-1967", Journal of Refugee Studies, Volume 25, Issue No. 3(2012), 407

protection from any state under international refugee law, they must first cross an internationally recognized border.[218]

Under the ambit of international refugee law, which concretised the centuries old practice of giving refuge to victims of violence and persecution, states have opened their borders to asylum seekers and given them protection. The rights and protections given to these asylum seekers has largely been governed by the states obligations as provided for under the aforementioned 1951 convention and also other major international conventions that contribute to the international refugee protection legal regime by providing guidelines on how states should administer refugee rights. Some of these conventions include: The Universal Declaration of Human Rights, The Geneva Convention Relative to the Protection of civilian persons in time of war, Protocol Additional to the Geneva Conventions and Relating to the Protection of Victims of International Conflicts, International Covenant on Civil and Political Rights (ICCPR), Convention against Torture and Other Cruel Inhuman or Degrading Treatment or Punishment, Convention on the Rights of the child, Declaration on the Elimination of Violence Against Women, African Charter on the Rights and Welfare of the Child, The Cartagena Declaration on Refugees and the Statute of the Office of the United Nations High Commissioner for Refugees. The existence of such extensive refugee protection regime could arguably be a demonstration of states intention to offer a helping hand to those who are considered the most vulnerable in the international society.

However, over the years, the numbers of asylum seekers have been on the rise and it has placed a huge socio-economic burden on the host communities. Host governments have faced internal criticisms for providing food and shelter to asylum seekers and refugees while its own citizens have gone hungry and slept in the cold. Further the cost implications that arise from refugee protection, such as refugee status processing and financial aid for basic needs has placed a great economic burden on some states particularly those considered to be developing states. Additionally, the events of September 11, 2001 in New York, the July 7, 2005 bombings in London and the recent attacks in various populated areas in Kenya have led to a great shift in state's willingness to allow refugee and asylum seekers into their territories. Drawing on the perception that there is an automatic link between asylum seekers and terrorism,[219] states worldwide have restricted access into their countries. This has led states to greatly favour a dynamic and flexible border concept

---

[218] Ibid, 408

[219] Anja Rudiger, "Prisoners of Terrorism? The impact of anti-terrorism measures on refugees and asylum seekers in Britain", A Refugee Council Report, (2007), 5

in order to ensure that they can effectively control who gets into their territories without being perceived to breach their international obligations.

States have argued that globalisation which promotes the 'erosion' of border restraints placed on immigration has greatly contributed to the ability of dangerous immigrants entering into their territories and causing harm to the citizens.[220] Therefore immigration policies have taken a drastic turn over the past several decades with states seeking to secure their 'broken borders' and ensure security risks are contained.[221] As Shachar argues states have sought to protect their borders by transforming them into something malleable which can be placed, by words of the law, in whatever location is thought to best suited to restricting access into the territory.[222] This is meant to enforce the sovereign prerogative to control access into the state in a bid to protect it and its citizens by regaining control of their borders.[223] These complex legal manoeuvres employed by the state enhance its authority to act against what it terms as 'unwanted intruders'.[224]

This rethinking of immigration policies has greatly affected asylum seekers and their ability to access protection from any given state. As mentioned earlier, legally the refugee and the asylum seeker are a construct of border crossing.[225] Since the affording of an asylum seeker of any rights or protection has been hinged on their presence in that state from which they are claiming protection, states wishing to prevent this will 'obstruct border crossings'.[226] Particularly in instances where there is a mass influx of refugees, states will seek to avert any costs and obligations that may arise from refugee protection by closing their borders and thus preventing them access into the state to claim protection.[227] The practice of border closures is a practice that is often associated with developing states and an example of this was demonstrated when Kenya closed its border with Somalia to prevent entry of any asylum seekers.[228] However these formal border closures are more associated with

---

[220] Shachar, The Shifting Border, 167
[221] Ibid
[222] Shachar, The Shifting Border, 167
[223] Shachar, The Shifting Border, 167; Randall Hansen, State Controls: Borders, Refugees, and Citizenship, in Elena Fiddian Qasmiyeh, Gil Loescher, Katy Long and Nando Sigona (eds.), *The Oxford Handbook of Refugee & Forced Migration Studies* (Oxford: Oxford University Press, 2014),258
[224] Shachar, The Shifting Border, 167
[225] Hansen, State Controls, 256
[226] Ibid, 258
[227] Hansen, State Controls, 258, 262; Katy Long, "In the Search of Sanctuary: Border Closures, 'Safe' Zones and Refugee Protection", Journal of Refugee Studies, Volume 26, Issue No. 3(2012), 462

the classical notion of the border as being a static and unchanging construct. Developed nations employ methods that manipulate rather than close their borders in order to avoid their obligations under the existing refugee framework.[229] Some of these methods that states have employed include the imposition of heavy fines to carriers found transporting those considered as illegal immigrants; the increased reliance on visas; extra-territorial processing of asylum seekers; excisions of their territories and also push backs at the sea to prevent entry.[230] These methods demonstrate how states have legally shifted their borders to extend either beyond the politically recognized territory of the state or to retract inwardly in relation to refugee migrations.

For instance, the concept of excision of territories is a demonstration of how a state can retract its border inwards and this was the method that was employed by the Australian Government in 2001. In August 2001, 439 Afghani asylum seekers aboard a Norwegian ship MV Tampa were denied entry into Australia with the government denying the ship permission to dock on Christmas Island which is part of its territory.[231] This situation garnered great global media coverage and resulted in a diplomatic row between Indonesia (the country where the ship was headed), Australia and Norway.[232] Thereafter Australia passed the Migration Amendment (Excision from Migration Zone) Act 2001 which was an amendment to the Migration Act of 1958.[233] This amendment to the act excised certain territories including Christmas Island, from what was termed as the Australian Immigration Zone.[234] As a result of this any non-citizen who, without any legal authorisation, entered Australia at any of the excised regions was prevented from applying for any visa including a protection visa unless the Australian Immigration Minister personally

---

[228] Long, In the Search of Sanctuary, 461; Katy Long, "No Entry! A review of UNHCR's response to border closures in situations of mass refugee influx", United Nations High Commissioner for Refugees Policy Development and Evaluation Service (PDES), (2010), 5

[229] Long, In the Search of Sanctuary, 461; Hansen, State Controls, 258

[230] Long, In the Search of Sanctuary, 461; Alice Edwards, "Tampering with Refugee Protection: The Case of Australia", International Journal of Refugee Law, Volume 15, Issue No. 2 (2003),193 ; Mariagiulia Giuffré, "State Responsibility Beyond Borders: What Legal Basis for Italy's Push-backs to Libya", International Journal of Refugee Law, Volume 24, Issue No. 4 (2013),693

[231] Refugee Council of Australia, "Timeline of major events in the history of Australia's Refugee and Humanitarian Program", at http://www.refugeecouncil.org.au/fact-sheets/australias-refugee-and-humanitarian-program/timeline/ (April 14 2015)

[232] Ibid
[233] Ibid
[234] Ibid

intervened to 'lift the bar'.[235] This arguably meant that if an asylum seeker illegally accessed Australia through any of these excised areas, for the purposes of migration, they were technically not in Australia and therefore could not apply for protection. Australia had constructed a border that related solely to migration; a border that was different from that that covered what was considered to be its territory on any political map. This legally constructed border reduced the government's responsibility to the asylum seeker and also limited the legal safeguards that such a person could access or that were guaranteed such as judicial review.[236] This same asylum seeker would more likely have had access to these legal safeguards had his port of entry been a city like Sydney or Perth because he would have been within the migration zone.[237] By this directive Australia could arguably be said to have essentially shifted is border inward and therefore demonstrated that in matters relating to migration and particularly refugee protection, its border was malleable thereby affirming Shachar's argument on the shifting border.

States also seek to shift their borders away from their recognized territorial frontiers to the territory of foreign countries. This is done in a bid to prevent the entry of unwanted migrants into the state's territory. States have found the reliance of visas as the best method of ensuring their migration laws and policies are enforced as through the visa application process, which takes place on foreign land, a state is able to intercept these unwanted migrants before they access that states territory.[238] This application process on foreign land is arguably the state extending its jurisdictional reach on migrants to beyond its borders.[239] However when it comes to refugees their reason for departure makes the visa processing at their country of origin impossible. States have however applied other methods to manipulate their borders to prevent access into their territory by the refugee. In order to curb the increased numbers of asylum seekers who were illegally making their way into Europe and putting a strain on state resources, the Dublin Convention was devised. The convention basically provides that all states that are a party to it consider each other to be safe third countries and provides a guideline on who ought to bear the

---

[235] [235] Refugee Council of Australia, "Timeline of major events in the history of Australia's Refugee and Humanitarian Program", http://www.refugeecouncil.org.au/fact-sheets/asylum-seeker-issues/excision/ (April 14 2015)

[236] Shachar, The Shifting Border, 173

[237] Anthea Vogl, "Over the Boderline: A Critical Inquiry into the Geography of Territorial Excision and the Securitisation of the Australian Border", University of New South Wales Law Journal, Volume 38, Issue No. 1 (2015), 114

[238] Shachar, The Shifting Border, 176

[239] Ibid, 175-176

responsibility processing an asylum seekers application.[240] The idea of a safe third country in relation to refugee protection usually refers to a state that an asylum seeker passed through on their way to the current state they are in. The former state is perceived to be capable of ensuring the protection of the asylum seeker and thus is considered by the current state as a safe third country. Thus the receiving state is able to return the asylum seeker to the country of transit for them to process within their own refugee status determination process. The concept of a safe third country in regard to application of the Dublin convention within Europe, essentially enables states to manage the flow of asylum seekers within their territories as it effectually allows pushing back asylum seekers to the first point of entry.[241] Shachar has described this as a border shifting strategy that has allowed the 'European Union to push its refugee-admission border to gate-keeper states to protect its core'.[242] This policy therefore 'creates a buffer zone around each country'[243] in the interior of Europe and moves enforcement mechanism to the continental perimeter which is now the 'new locus for the exercise of legal authority'.[244] This arrangement is hugely beneficial to the states in the hinterland but places a large burden on the states that are situated at the continental perimeter. They potentially bear the greatest responsibility to provide protection for asylum seekers that accesses Europe through them. This places considerable pressure on these countries thus causing them to employ border shifting tactics of their own. This was evidenced in 2009 when Italy, in a bid to tackle the issue of illegal immigration by sea, employed it push-back policy for asylum seekers from North Africa seeking to gain entry into Europe.[245] Through this controversial policy Italy forcibly and indiscriminately returned and deflected hundreds of people back into North Africa before they could enter any EU member state's territorial waters.[246] Italian authorities, without providing an opportunity for application for asylum, intercepted these asylum seekers on the high seas and returned them to Libya.[247] The asylum seekers intercepted in the course of their journey were transferred onto Italian vessels from their unseaworthy boats and transported back to Libya where they were forced to disembark.[248] Italy in this instance considered Libya as safe haven for asylum

---

[240] Agnès Hurwitz, *The Collective Responsibility of States to Protect Refugees* (Oxford: Oxford University Press, 2009), 89
[241] Shachar, The Shifting Border, 178
[242] Ibid
[243] Ibid
[244] Ibid
[245] Guiffré, State Responsibility Beyond Borders, 693
[246] Ibid
[247] Ibid, 694

seekers and thus transferred its potential responsibility over these asylum seekers onto it.[249] By adopting the concept of the safe third country and transferring the asylum seekers to the custody of another state, the sending state is arguably demonstrating that it is has extinguished its responsibility and legal obligation over that individual. In actual fact the concept of the safe third state arguably shifts the border far beyond the territory of that state and with it extends the reach of that state's responsibility over asylum seekers. This is because a country must evaluate a third country's safety policies in respect of asylum seekers in order to extinguish its responsibility under international law. Consequently, any border control measures taken by states at the territorial border of the continent 'must be measured against international and European legal standards' of refugee protection.[250] The states involved in these safe third country agreement arrangements therefore extend their responsibility far beyond their own territorial border.

Through these tactics illustrated above states have taken to adjust their migration borders in order to limit the reach of or do away with their responsibilities under international refugee law. However, as shall be discussed below, these tactics of border manipulation have not diminished their obligations as expected and in some instance, it has extended the reach of their obligation beyond their own physical territories.

## Unchanged Obligations

With the rising state of insecurity in the post 9/11 world, it is understandable that states would take aggressive measures to protect themselves. One way for a state to increase security is to control and monitor who can access their borders and gain entry into their territory. In a bid to do this the easiest targets are usually those who are already considered social pariahs in any state; the illegal immigrant. In fact Hammerstad notes that in the recent past, there has been a systematic inclusion of various categories of migrants such as refugees and asylum seekers into the numerous security scholars' research agendas.[251] This perhaps can be attributed to the fact that it is difficult for the state to monitor illegal immigrants as it is essentially unaware of their existence within their territory and thus their security

---

[248] Ibid, 697
[249] Ibid, 700
[250] Andreas Fischer-Lescano, Tillmann Löhr & Timo Tohidipur, "Border Controls at Sea: Requirements under International Human Rights and Refugee Law", International Journal of Refugee Law, Volume 21, Issue No. 2 (2009),257
[251] Anne Hammerstad, The Securitization of Forced Migration, in Elena Fiddian Qasmiyeh, Gil Loescher, Katy Long and Nando Sigona (eds.), *The Oxford Handbook of Refugee & Forced Migration Studies* (Oxford: Oxford University Press, 2014), 265

threat level cannot be accurately assessed. Further, even though the illegal immigrant may gain entry into a state with the noblest of intentions of improving their economic well-being, their mode of illegal entry poses a threat to the security of the state as a potential terrorist may employ the same method to access the state. One way that illegal immigrants seek to gain entry into most developed states is to fraudulently claim asylum. These attempts to manipulate a state's asylum system could be argued to leads to a high level of asylum seekers which in turn puts a financial strain on the asylum processing systems of the state. Since the state has a responsibility to protect potential refugees, it may be placed in a difficult position when persons present fraudulent documentation in order to gain entry and be granted protection. So the easiest solution for any state is to limit entry into the state by any illegal immigrants regardless of whether or not they are genuine asylum seekers. This could debatably be the justification by developed states to put in place the border manipulation tactics described above. This is perhaps the only way that they can ensure that anybody who gains access into their territory has been granted permission to be there, preferably before they get to the territorial border.

The problem with this method of curbing illegal immigration is that the genuine asylum seekers and refugees are unfairly denied protection and a state fails to adhere to its obligations under the 1951 Convention. States employing these methods of border manipulation to deal with illegal immigrants gaining access into their territory is a demonstration of a state seeking to avoid responsibility owed to legitimate refugees.[252] In the course of their flight from danger refugees will obviously have no time for immigration formalities and that is why it is understood that their legal status under the aliens or immigration law of their state in which they are claiming protection is irrelevant.[253] This exemption to fulfil the immigration requirements of the state they have fled to is provided for under article 31 of the convention.[254] Article 31(1) provides that so long as the refugee presents himself to the authorities without delay and shows good cause for their illegal presence or entry, then the state is under an obligation not to impose any penalties on the said refugee as a result of his illegal entry.[255] More often than not the imposition of penalties in this respect will be done without due consideration of the merits of the individuals claim thus violating the state's obligation to ensure the protection of all who are present it its territory or 'subject to its jurisdiction'.[256]

---

[252] Guy S. Goodwin-Gill, *The Refugee in International Law: Second Edition* (Oxford: Oxford University Press, 1998), 152
[253] Ibid
[254] Ibid
[255] Convention relating to the Status of Refugees 1951
[256] Guy S. Goodwin-Gill, Article 31 of the 1951 Convention Relating to the Status

Though the understanding of what is considered as illegal entry is generally agreed upon,[257] what is understood as penalties has been subject to great debate.[258] Since it is not defined in the convention the debate has been whether or not a limited interpretation should be applied to encompass criminal penalties only or should it be expansive enough to include administrative penalties.[259] It has been generally understood that the since the main object of the article is to prevent castigation on account of illegal entry, a broader interpretation that includes but is not limited to fines, prosecution and imprisonment should be applied.[260] With the understanding that the lack of the definition of the term coupled with the purpose of the article, the Social Security Commissioner, in the United Kingdom, on hearing an appeal filed held that 'any treatment that was less favourable than that accorded to others and was imposed on account of illegal entry' should be considered as penalty under article 31(1) unless the same could be objectively justified on administrative grounds.[261] In light of the foregoing definition, when one then considers the decision by the Australian Government to refuse to grant protection visas to *de facto* refugees under the Convention, it is clear that this was a penalty that was being imposed unfairly due to their mode of entry into the state. Due to the position that Australia had placed them, they were treated differently from those who were legally within the Australian migration zone. They were also treated differently from those who arrived legally within these excised regions. Therefore, purely based on their illegal entry they were not only ineligible to apply for protection visas, but also unable to access the courts or any judicial review mechanism if the state decides to expel them from the region. In the absence of an objective administration justification as to why these *de facto* refugees were treated differently due to their illegal entry, this treatment was a violation of Australia's obligation under this article. Since the government continues to exercise administrative jurisdiction over the persons in these excised areas by determining their status and the fact that it has not lodged any reservations as to which of its territories the convention applies,[262] it is estopped from claiming

---

of Refugees: non-penalization, detention, and protection, in Erika Feller, Volker Türk and Frances Nicholson (eds.), *Refugee Protection in International Law: UNHCR's Global Consultations on International Protection* (Cambridge: Cambridge University Press, 2003), 187

[257] Goodwin-Gill, Article 31, 196
[258] Ibid, 193-196
[259] Ibid, 194
[260] Ibid, 195;219
[261] Decision of the Social Security Commissioner in Case No. CIS 4439/98 [25 November 1999] at www.rightsnet.org.uk/pdfs/cmmr_upload/cis/cis443998.doc (14 April 2015), paragraph 16; Goodwin-Gill, Article 31, 204; 209
[262] Edwards, Tampering with Refugee Protection, 194

that its obligations under the convention do not extend to the excised regions. It consequently appears that its efforts to manipulate its border do not affect the scope of its obligations in this regard and as such it is still bound to protect all those arriving within its territory.

The question of whether or not a state's obligations persist also arises when one considers the push-back tactics of potentially genuine refugees particularly when they occur at the high seas. When this rejection occurs within the territorial waters of the state as was seen with Italy in 2009, then this amounts to a violation of the states' obligation of *non-refoulement* as provided for under Article 33 of the convention. The article provides that contracting states are obliged not to return or expel (refouler) a refugee to the frontiers of territories where their life or freedom would be threatened. The article enshrines this principle of *non-refoulement* which is now considered principle under international customary law.[263] The principle applies to all refugees regardless of whether or not they have been formally recognised as such by the state they are in.[264] The debate that has often surrounded the issue of *non-refoulement* is whether it applies only to those who have already entered state territory thus leaving the state with the possibility of rejecting those at the frontier. State practice has however demonstrated that the moment an asylum seeker presents himself for entry, the principle of *non-refoulement* is engaged.[265] Therefore states are not at liberty to reject genuine asylum seekers at the frontier unless they have adopted a course of action that will not be considered to amount to *refoulement*; a course of action that ensures they are protected elsewhere.[266] In fact it has been argued that 'anyone who presents themselves at a frontier' of a state will already be within that state's territory and jurisdiction.[267] Thus Italy's push-backs when they occurred within their territorial waters were in violation of that state's obligation of *non-refoulement* in respect to the genuine asylum seekers aboard those vessels. When it comes to push backs that happened in international waters however, most states argue that when such border control activities occur at high seas, they do so in a space where both human rights and refugee law are inapplicable.[268] This position has been pivoted on the decision by the United States Supreme Court decision in *Sale*

---

[263] Elihu Lauterpacht and Daniel Bethlehem, The scope and content of the principle of non-refoulement Opinion, in Erika Feller, Volker Türk and Frances Nicholson (eds.), *Refugee Protection in International Law: UNHCR's Global Consultations on International Protection* (Cambridge: Cambridge University Press, 2003), 178
[264] Lauterpacht and Bethlehem, Non-Refoulement, 178
[265] Goodwin-Gill, The Refugee in International Law, 123-124
[266] Lauterpacht and Bethlehem, Non-Refoulement, 113
[267] Goodwin-Gill, The Refugee in International Law, 123
[268] Fischer-Lescano et al., Border Controls at Sea, 257; 265

*v. Haitian Centers Council* case where the court ruled that the government's position to force Haitian refugee boats physically out of US territorial waters was lawful citing that article 33(1) does not have extraterritorial effect.[269] However this position has been rejected as being purely political and not legally sound.[270] Since the objective of the convention is arguably to provide protection against persecution related abuses in the country of origin, placing a territorial restriction on its application would frustrate its purpose.[271] It is has consequently been accepted that outside the refugee's own country of origin, there can be no place where the principle of *non-refoulement* does not apply, inclusive of those areas declared as international zones.[272] This ensures that the refugee is not placed in a position where they are exposed to or risk persecution.[273] The applicability of this principle extraterritorially is also further supported by the UNHCR prohibition on states from 'reading geographical restrictions into rules of the convention containing no such limitations'.[274] Thus through push backs at the high sea Italy arguably extended its administrative migration border well beyond its own territory. However, despite its best efforts to avoid responsibility, it was still in violation of its obligations under the convention.

These violations ought to be considered when any other country within the European continent classifies Italy as a safe third country. When the European states, through the Dublin convention, manipulated their borders and essentially moved it to the continental perimeter, they did so on the mutual recognition that all the states were safe third countries. The essence of the concept of the safe third country is to ensure protection of the refugee in another state other than the state they are currently claiming protection from. However that country must be capable of providing protection to the refugee by ensuring non-persecution of the individual, freedom from torture and cruel treatment, and it must also respect the principle of *non-refoulement*.[275] This is essential because the only way to guarantee that a state action of sending a refugee back to the state of transit does not amount to *refoulement* is the recognition of that state as a safe third country.[276] This is the same position that ought to have been adopted by Italy in its consideration of Libya as a safe third country. When states enter into safe third country agreements with other

---

[269] Ibid, 266
[270] Ibid, 268
[271] Ibid, 269
[272] Fischer-Lescano et al., Border Controls at Sea, 267-8
[273] Ibid, 268
[274] Ibid, 270
[275] "Section 12: The Safe Third Country Concept" at http://www.refworld.org/cgi-bin/texis/vtx/rwmain/opendocpdf.pdf?reldoc=y&docid=4bab55e22 (April 18 2015)
[276] Lauterpacht and Bethlehem, Non-Refoulement, 113

states they may shift border, but they extend their responsibilities in that they need to ensure that the rights of that individual are respected in that state in order to satisfy their own obligation of *non-refoulement*. Though the state may create a buffer for itself in that it does not have to absorb the financial responsibilities that come with refugee protection by transferring the refugee to another state, its obligations to ensuring the protection of that refugee remain unchanged. Therefore, whatever measures a state takes under the guise of border control it must ensure its obligations toward genuine refugees are upheld regardless.[277]

## Conclusion

The border is a fundamental piece of the puzzle in determining who is or is not a refugee. It is also the point at which a state's obligation to a refugee attaches. Recognizably the constant state of conflict in various regions of the world has led to an increase in the numbers of refugees. This has inevitably placed a burden on states with them having to bear the great costs that are associated with refugee protection. Additionally, in the post 9/11 world we live in asylum seekers have come to be mistakenly identified as either being terrorists or terrorist sympathizers. This status quo has led to states adopting various methods to avoid having to deal with these asylum seekers within their territories. By adopting the understanding that their border is flexible and not static, they have taken to implementing border manipulation tactics to avoid responsibility under international refugee law. By shifting their borders, they have sought to establish where and when their obligation to protect asylum seekers begins. However, in this paper I have sought to demonstrate that their border shifting tactics are an exercise in futility as their responsibility to protect persists regardless. They therefore now have an even greater responsibility to ensure that whatever measures are taken to curb illegal migration, they must ensure that their responsibility to protect the asylum seeker is not compromised in anyway.

## References

Agnès Hurwitz, The Collective Responsibility of States to Protect Refugees (Oxford: Oxford University Press, 2009)

Alice Edwards, "Tampering with Refugee Protection: The Case of Australia", International Journal of Refugee Law, Volume 15, Issue No. 2 (2003), 192-211

Andreas Fischer-Lescano, Tillmann Löhr & Timo Tohidipur, "Border Controls at Sea: Requirements under International Human Rights and Refugee Law", International Journal of Refugee Law, Volume 21, Issue No. 2 (2009), 256-296

---

[277] Giuffré, State Responsibility Beyond Borders, 708

Anja Rudiger, "Prisoners of Terrorism? The impact of anti-terrorism measures on refugees and asylum seekers in Britain", A Refugee Council Report, (2007)

Anthea Vogl, "Over the Boderline: A Critical Inquiry into the Geography of Territorial Excision and the Securitisation of the Australian Border", University of New South Wales Law Journal, Volume 38, Issue No. 1 (2015), 114-145

Ayelet Shachar, "The Shifting Border of Immigration Regulation", Stanford Journal of Civic Rights and Civil Liberties, Volume 3, (2007), 165-193

Decision of the Social Security Commissioner in Case No. CIS 4439/98 [25 November 1999] at www.rightsnet.org.uk/pdfs/cmmr_upload/cis/cis443998.doc (14 April 2015)

Efrat Arbel, "Shifting Borders and the Boundaries of Rights: Examining the Safe Third Country Agreement between Canada and the United States", International Journal of Refugee Law, Volume 25, Issue No. 1 (2013), 65-86

Elena Fiddian Qasmiyeh, Gil Loescher, Katy Long and Nando Sigona (eds.), The Oxford Handbook of Refugee & Forced Migration Studies (Oxford: Oxford University Press, 2014)

Erika Feller, Volker Türk and Frances Nicholson (eds.), Refugee Protection in International Law: UNHCR's Global Consultations on International Protection (Cambridge: Cambridge University Press, 2003)

Guy S. Goodwin-Gill, The Refugee in International Law: Second Edition (Oxford: Oxford University Press, 1998)

Katy Long, "In the Search of Sanctuary: Border Closures, 'Safe' Zones and Refugee Protection", Journal of Refugee Studies, Volume 26, Issue No. 3(2012), 458-476

Katy Long, "No Entry! A review of UNHCR's response to border closures in situations of mass refugee influx", United Nations High Commissioner for Refugees Policy Development and Evaluation Service (PDES), (2010)

Laura Madokoro, "Borders Transformed: Sovereign Concerns, Population Movements and the Making of Territorial Frontiers in Hong Kong, 1949-1967", Journal of Refugee Studies, Volume 25, Issue No. 3(2012), 407-427

Mariagiulia Giuffré, "State Responsibility Beyond Borders: What Legal Basis for Italy's Push-backs to Libya", International Journal of Refugee Law, Volume 24, Issue No. 4 (2013), 692-734

OAU Convention Governing the Specific Aspects of Refugee Problems in Africa (1969)

Refugee Council of Australia, "Timeline of major events in the history of Australia's Refugee and Humanitarian Program", at http://www.refugeecouncil.org.au/fact-sheets/australias-refugee-and-humanitarian-program/timeline/ (April 14 2015)

The Convention relating to the Status of Refugees (1951)

Veronika Magyar-Haas, "Ambivalent Concepts of the Border: Political Borders – Bodily Boundaries", Social Work and Society International Online Journal, Volume 10, Issue No. 2 (2012), at http://www.socwork.net/sws/article/view/336/673 (April 14 2015)

# Resolving Disputes Of Land As A Peacebuilding Project:

Is the Bosnian model applicable to other post-conflict societies?

## Azra Hodzic

*This essay discusses reasons behind the success of property restitution using Bosnia and Hercegovina as a case study, and if the Bosnian model can be used in other post-conflict countries as a peacebuilding project. It has been 20 years since the conflict in Bosnia and Hercegovina ended; a destructive ethnical conflict in which thousands of people lost their lives and half of the population – 2.2 million people – were forced to flee their homes. A legal process of returning property to more than 200 000 refugees began as the war had ended in 1995; all 2.2 million displaced have been given an opportunity to return to their homes and municipalities, meeting the main criteria in the General Framework Agreement for Peace. This large-scale post-conflict restitution process, known in Bosnia and Hercegovina as "property law implementation" stands as a landmark model in the history of international peace building, due to strong presence of the international community, property rights and length of displacement. However, this essay calls into question if the Bosnian model can be applicable in other post-conflict countries due to different legal sources and justification of rights.*

## Introduction

In many conflicts around the world, land, property and other possessions, are widely recognised as 'spoils of war' by the victors. Although the law of armed conflict expressly, prohibits the arbitrary destruction and expropriation of property, the right of people who fled their homes due to conflict was largely ignored in practice. Humanitarian agencies and governments invest their efforts in providing shelter and addressing the immediate needs of refugees and internally displaced.

While the basic right to land and property is clear, many of the issues regarding solving disputes of land are complex. In many instances, houses have been ruined, occupied by 'secondary' occupants or abandoned. Official records of ownership may have been destroyed or appear incorrect. In other cases, some may have felt 'compelled' to sell their property or resided on property, which over time has been recognised as theirs through customary law.

Sorting out these issues, in a post-conflict society, with weak state institutions and widely spread corruption remains a difficult challenge. In 2005, the UN Sub – Commission on the Promotion and Protection of Human Rights approved a set of international regulations on Housing and Restitution for Refugees and Displaced Persons known as the Pinheiro Principles. The principles reflect much of the work conducted on this field worldwide; however, one country in specific stands out, Bosnia and Hercegovina.

The international community first attempt to tackle the issue of property restitution came during the war in the former Yugoslavia. The Bosnian model in regard to property and land restitution is today recognised as a 'landmark model' in the international community, when it comes to solving disputes of land. This essay's objective is to discuss to what extent this particular model can be used in other post – conflict societies on property restitution, and which lessons can be learned from the Bosnian model.

Following the introduction, this essay will discuss the sources of property restitution in international law, then explain the role of the High Representative in the process and laws which played a role in the restitution process, explain the importance of the rule of law approach in peacebuilding, and discuss the applicability of the model to other post-conflict societies.

## Sources Of Property Restitution In International Law

The right of refugees and internally displaced persons to return to their homes and return to their country of origin in the aftermath of conflict, has developed as a human rights norm over the last decade. International peacekeeping missions recognise the need for property restitution, as returning back to the country or origin and 'home', are indispensable corners of peace, prosperity, development and reconciliation in war-torn countries. Rhodri C. Williams argues, that under international human rights law, property restitution is a necessary measure to create conditions for refugee return, and (or) remedy for human rights violations. 'Dual source' for restitution can complicate the process of implementation and scholars do not provide a 'straight forward' answer on this matter; however, in the case of Bosnia and Hercegovina, the focus on 'rights-based' restitution instead of 'return-based' was the key, from both the international and local level, that unlocked the challenges connected to property restitution[278].

The 'right to return' is a principle drawn from the UN Declaration on Human Rights, article 13 (2)[279], later recognised in The International Covenant for Civil and Political rights, Article 12 (4) "No one shall be arbitrarily deprived of the right to enter his own country"[280], intended to encourage people to re-enter and return to their country of origin. The 1951 Convention Relating to the Status of Refugees (with its 1967 Additional Protocol) does not mention the right to return, but mentions in Article 33 (1), that refugees shall not be returned to countries where they face danger, known as the principle of non – refoulement[281].

The General Framework Agreement for Peace, which ended the conflict in Bosnia and Hercegovina in 1995, was the first international agreement to set forth the 'right to return home' and not only to the country, but back to one's own property and land[282]. The right to housing is recognised in a number of international human rights instruments. Article 25 (1) of the Universal Declaration on Human Rights recognises the right to housing[283]. Article 11 (1) of the International Covenant on Economic, Social and Cultural Rights mentions the right to housing as part of an adequate

---

[278] Rhodri C. Williams, Post-Conflict Property Restitution and Refugee Return in Bosnia and Hercegovina:
Implications for International Standard-Setting and Practice, New York University Journal of International Law and Politics, Vol. 37 No.3 (2005), 441-553, see pp. 451- 452.
[279] UN Declaration on Human Rights (UDHR); Article 13 (2) "Everyone has the right to leave any country, including his own, and to return to his country".
[280] International Covenant on Civil and Political Rights (ICCPR), Article 12 (4).
[281] 1951 Convention Relating to the Status of Refugees, Article 33 (1)." No Contracting State shall expel or return ("refouler") a refugee in any manner whatsoever to the frontiers of territories where his life or freedom would be threatened on account of his race, religion, nationality, membership of a particular social group or political opinion".
[282] Mari Katayanagi, Property Restitution and the Rule of Law in Peacebuilding: Examining the Applicability of the Bosnian model, Paper prepared for presentation at the 2014 World Bank Conference On Land And Poverty The World Bank - Washington DC, March 24-27, 2014, see page 7.
[283] UNHR, Article 25 (1) "Everyone has the right to a standard of living adequate for the health and well-being of himself and of his family, including food, clothing, housing and medical care and necessary social services, and the right to security in the event of unemployment, sickness, disability, widowhood, old age or other lack of livelihood in circumstances beyond his control".

standard of living[284]. In the General Framework Agreement, the right to return and housing is mentioned in Annex 4 "The Constitution", Article II (5), "All refugees and displaced persons have the right freely to return to their homes of origin"[285], and in Annex 7 the agreement on Refugees and Internally Displaced persons. Article 1(1) in Annex 7 is identical with Article II (5) in Annex 4[286], recognising the early return of refugees and internally displaced, as a necessary measure in the settlement between the parties of Bosnia and Hercegovina.

Article 1(1) in the General Framework Agreement for Peace continues to say that all refugees and internally displaced "shall have the right to have restored to them property of which they were deprived in the course of hostilities since 1991 and to be compensated for any property that cannot be restored to them"[287]. Giving refugees and internally displaced an opportunity to go back to their home, was an objective in reversing ethnical cleansing and create a multi-ethnic society in a divided country.

During the early 90's, nearly 2,2 million people were forced to leave their homes in Bosnia and Hercegovina. A total of 1.2 million people left the country, while 1 million people remained within the borders[288]. The 1992 – 1995 conflict, took place as a result of the collapse of the former Yugoslavia between the three ethnic groups of the country; Bosnian Croats, Bosnian Muslims and the Bosnian Serb. The ethnic conflict ended in 1995 with the signing of the Dayton accords, also known as the General Framework Agreement for Peace. The agreement created a new state composed of two federal units; The Federation of Bosnia and Hercegovina, consisting of mostly Bosnian Croats and Bosnian Muslims, and the Serb dominated Republika Srpska.

---

[284] International Covenant for Economic, Social and Cultural Rights (ICESCR), Article 11 (1) "The States Parties to the present Covenant recognize the right of everyone to an adequate standard of living for himself and his family, including adequate food, clothing and housing, and to the continuous improvement of living conditions. The States Parties will take appropriate steps to ensure the realization of this right, recognizing to this effect the essential importance of international co-operation based on free consent".

[285] The General Framework for Peace (GFA); Annex 4 "Constitution of Bosnia and Hercegovina, Article II (5) "Human Rights and Fundamental Freedoms" see http://www.ohr.int/?page_id=63255

[286] Ibid, Annex 7 «Agreement on Refugees and Displaced Persons», Article 1 (1) "Rights of Refugees and Displaced Persons" see http://www.ohr.int/?page_id=63261

[287] Ibid.

[288] Bosnian Ministry of Human Rights and Refugees (BMHRR), Comparative Analysis on Access to Right to Refugees and Displaced Persons (September 2005), available at http://www.mhrr.gov.ba/PDF/default.aspx?id=283&langTag=bs-BA See pages 23-24 (Viewed 20.04.15).

Property and particularly land, have been subject to power in Bosnia and Hercegovina, often linked to ethno-politics. Under the Ottoman Empire, land tenure belonged to the Sultan, the big land-owners were Muslims and most peasants were of Christian faith. The feudal relations changed, transferring land to the poorer peasants, with the first land reform in 1918 and then with second land reform in 1945, during the regime of Josip Broz Tito[289].

Due to the nature of the conflict in Bosnia and Hercegovina, many houses and properties were destroyed, neglected or occupied by 'secondary' occupants. The Bosnian Ministry for Human Rights and Refugees estimate that 452 000 housing units were destroyed during the conflict from 1992-1995[290]. The return of refugees and displaced persons was understood as the key to achieve political stability. The peace agreement specified the parties to take the necessary steps, including property restitution and facilitate homes for the internally displaced[291].

## The Role Of The High Representative

The UNCHR has been the leading organisation regarding the return issue itself; however, the Office of the High Representative (OHR) is monitoring all aspects of the implementation process of the General Framework Agreement for Peace, including property restitution. The General Framework Agreement for Peace, contains the constitution of Bosnia and Hercegovina, provides for the military presence in the country and creates the legal basis for The High Representative[292].

The United Nations Security Council adopted in December 1995, resolution 1031. The Council, acting under Chapter VII of the charter, discussed the transfer of authority from the United Nations Protection Force (UNPROFOR) to the multinational implementation force (IFOR). In this regard, the Council re-affirmed the post of the High Representative created by the Dayton accords, to monitor the implementation of the peace treaty[293]. The High Representative is nominated by the

---

[289] Katayanagi, pp. 5 and 6.
[290] BMHRR, p. 63.
[291] GFA: Annex 7, Article 1 (3).
[292] Office of the High Representative, "General Information" available at http://www.ohr.int/?page_id=1139 (Viewed at 13.08.16).
[293] UNSC resolution 1031 (1995), para 26: "Endorses the establishment of a High Representative, following the request of the parties, who, in accordance with Annex 10 on the civilian implementation of the Peace Agreement, will monitor the implementation of the Peace Agreement and mobilize and, as appropriate, give guidance to, and coordinate the activities of, the civilian organizations and agencies involved, and agrees the designation of Mr. Carl Bildt as High Representative".

Peace Implementation Council (donors to the peace implementation process), and the UN Security Council endorses the High Representative's nomination[294].

The High Representative's mandate is stipulated in Annex 10, Article II (1 )of the agreement, which involves (b) "maintain close contact with the parties", (c) "coordinate activities", (d) "facilitate" (e) "participate" (f)" report periodically" (g) "provide guidance". Article II grants the High Representative authority to create, amend or dismiss any new legislation under the instrument[295]. The High Representative has no authority over the military forces in Bosnia and Hercegovina[296]. It is worth noting that the High Representative does not specifically work for the United Nations or any other international organisation; merely, represent the commitments the international community has in Bosnia and Hercegovina.

The High Representative is conferred with more powers than the constitution itself and can override it. This power is stipulated in Annex 10, Article V "The High Representative is the final authority in theatre regarding interpretation of this Agreement on the civilian implementation of the peace settlement"[297]. Article 5 to Annex 10 is re-affirmed by the UN Security Council resolution 1031, paragraph 27[298], this gives the High Representative the final say in regards to interpretation of on the civilian implementation of the peace. This specific authority is known as the Bonn powers, and has played an important role in property restitution in Bosnia and Hercegovina[299].

## Establishing Ownership

In pre-conflict Bosnia and Hercegovina, there were pre-dominantly two categories of residential property. The majority of homes were possessed as private property and the rest (approximately 20 %) were state property, known as social housing[300].

---

[294] See homepage of OHR.

[295] GFA; Annex 10, Article II, "The High Representative shall (a)monitor, (b)maintain, (c)coordinate, (d)facilitate, (e)participate, (f)report, (g)provide"

[296] Ibid, Annex 10, Article II (9).

[297] Ibid, Annex 10, Article V.

[298] UNSC resolution 1031, para 27 "Confirms that the High Representative is the final authority in theatre regarding interpretation of Annex 10 on the civilian implementation of the Peace Agreement".

[299] The Peace Implementation Council meet in Bonn in 1997, to review the progress of the Dayton Accords. It resulted in 'empowering' the High Representative, as the authorities in Bosnia and Hercegovina were not meeting their responsibilities. See PIC BONN conclusions, Article XI. High Representative.

[300] Williams, p. 478. Compared to other socialist states, the SFRY had a higher percentage of private owned houses, which signifies the limited control the state had

State owned apartments were built by larger state enterprises or other state institutions for allocation to their employees, who became the 'occupancy right holder'. All the citizens of Socialist Federation Republic of Former Yugoslavia (SFYR) were required to pay a fee, based on their income, to subsidise housing construction and in maintaining of public facilities. The rights of both the public bodies that formally owned the property (allocation right holder) and the occupancy right holder, were regulated by laws on housing relations that were largely identical in all the former Yugoslavian Republics. In accordance with the SRBiH Law on Housing Relations from 1959, an occupancy right to an apartment, once allocated, entitled the occupancy right holder to lifelong use of the apartment[301].

These rights were family based, meaning property and house were not considered belonging to one individual, spouses living together, or other family members were also considered as the 'occupancy' right holder. The law secured tenure for all family members, providing women and men equal rights and transferring of rights by death[302].

As hostilities erupted throughout the country in 1992, ethnic minorities fled to areas controlled by 'their own' ethnic group, leaving their own homes, and in a need for a new home in areas where they were displaced. The parties to the conflict were quick to adopt procedures, allowing the homes, both private and state owned, of those who had fled to be declared 'abandoned' and allocated for use by internally displaced or by those in power[303].

During the conflict, throughout the country, high number of abandoned apartments were considered to be 'abandoned', if the pre-right holder did not return to their property within seven days (15 days if one had crossed the border to another country), a policy which was regulated under the 'Law on Abandoned Property and Law of Housing Relations' - thus cancelling the pre-war 'occupancy right'. This right continued after the war had ended in 1995[304]. In January 1996, Republika Srpska passed the 'Law on the Use of Abandoned Property', which legitimized the

---

in controlling housing. This limited control was especially visible in the phenomenon 'black market'. Professor Mina Petrović argues that the social policy regarding housing, was created on a system that favoured the elites of the country, a policy that was taken advantage of by all parties, during the war, in an effort get control over the territory.

[301] Ibid, p. 479.
[302] UN-Habitat, Housing and Property Rights in Bosnia and Hercegovina, Croatia and Serbia and Montenegro (2005), see chapter 2, page 22.
[303] Williams, pp. 484-485.
[304] Ibid.

use of abandoned homes until temporary occupants re-possessed their own homes or had been compensated for the loss of their property[305].

In many post-conflict societies, one of the biggest challenges in regard to how to solve the question of housing, is the right to require previously owned property. Many 'temporary' or 'secondary' users of the property they reside on, have nowhere else to turn to, nor have a home to return to. This involves the home they once possessed, which either has been destroyed during the conflict or been occupied by someone else in the same position as themselves. The state they are the citizens of before the conflict, does not have the mechanisms or the resources, to solve their question of property; so, how does one address these challenges? To whom does one turn to? Can we assume that it is safe for refugees and internally displaced to return 'home'?

## Understanding The Scope Of The Restitution Rights

The immediate effect of the General Framework Agreement for Peace Annex 7 did not involve the return of refugees and internally displaced *en masse* as one would have thought. The effect of the laws and regulations in relation to the use of abandoned property, continued in the time after 1995. The BiH Human Rights Chamber noted in 1999, that these laws were part of a discriminatory policy to discourage people from returning to their homes and enjoying their possessions[306]. One aspect was the fact that people were under the impression they could not return home; another aspect was the rising pressure of the 700,000 refugees, residing in many European countries, who were slowly returning back to Bosnia and Hercegovina, and who were starting to re-claim their property[307].

In an effort to deal with the 'temporary use' of property throughout Bosnia and Hercegovina, the international community, under The High Representative, came to focus on repealing all regulations on abandoned property and replacing them with administrative restitution procedures[308]. Both entities, the Federation of Bosnia and

---

[305] Law on Use of Abandoned Property, Official Gazette of the Republika Srpska, Nos. 3/96, 21/96. See also The institution of Human Rights Ombudsman in Bosnia and Hercegovina, Special Report of the Ombudsman in BiH dealing with abandoned property in BiH, 24 May 2012, available at
http://www.ombudsmen.gov.ba/documents/obmudsmen_doc2013020406405420eng.pdf See page 3.

[306] Case No. CH/98/659: Pletili´c and others. against Republika Srpska, Decision on Request for Review, Human Rights Chamber in Bosnia and Hercegovina (September 10, 1999), available at http://www.hrc.ba/database/decisions/CH98-659%20et%20al%20Pletilic%20et%20al%20Request%20for%20review%20E.pdf para 24.

[307] Williams, p. 489.

[308] Ibid.

Hercegovina and the Republika Srpska, adopted laws to regulate abandoned property. In April 1998, the Federation passed one law dealing with private property, the 'Law on Cessation of the Application of the Law on Temporarily Abandoned Real Property Owned by Citizens'[309], and one for socially owned apartments, the 'Law on the Cessation of the Application of the Law on Abandoned Apartments'[310]. Republika Srpska followed in December 1998 and passed the law 'Cessation of the Application of the Law on the Use of Abandoned Property', which both dealt with private and socially owned property'[311].

The 'Laws of Cessation' are referred to as 'restitution laws' and were the first step in the property restitution process. There are many reasons why these laws played a central role in Bosnia and Hercegovina. They represented an important shift in that they cancelled wartime transactions with the presumption that all transactions had taken place under pressure. They also established a domestic administrative process by which pre-war owners and occupancy right holders could claim to return home to their pre-war property[312]. The laws established which rights proceeded and who the property belonged to. The Law on Cessation is identical in both entities and stipulates as following[313]:

> *"The owner, possessor or user of the real property who abandoned the property shall have the right to repossess the real property with all the rights which s/he had before 30 April 1991 or before the real property became abandoned".*

The laws recognised the 'rights' holder as those who had been in possession of property before the conflict in 1992. The administrative process handled cases in which the property had been reallocated specifically by wartime legislation. Cases in which the property had been occupied, or had not been reallocated, came under the jurisdiction of the courts until The High Representative amended the law in October

---

[309] FBH Official Gazette, no. 11/98. See also Office of the High Representative, "Decision on the Instruction on Application of the Law on Cessation of Application of the Law on Abandoned Apartments in its amended form", available at http://www.ohr.int/?p=67665 See para 6.
[310] Ibid,
[311] RS Official Gazette, no. 38/98. See also the Office of the High Representative, "Cessation of the Application of the Law on the Use of Abandoned Property", available at http://www.ohr.int/?p=65812 See article 3.
[312] Charles B. Philpott, From the Right to Return to the Return of Rights: Complementing Post-War Property Restitution in Bosnia and Hercegovina, International Journal of Refugee Law, Vol. 18 No.1 (2006), 30-80, see page 41-42.
[313] RS Official Gazette, no 38/39. See Office of the High Representative, Article 3.

1999, to bring these cases under the courts, speeding up the process of the restitution process[314].

In the process of reviewing the applications, the CRPC (Commission for Real Property Claims of Displaced Persons and Refugees) was established by the General Framework Agreement for Peace under Annex 6, to address disputes on property issues[315]. The committee consisted of nine members; three international members, four members from the Federation of Bosnia and Hercegovina, and two from Republika Srpska, to secure neutrality[316]. The CRPC was the body established with the specific purpose in handling property claims. Annex 7 gave it power to disregard any illegal property transactions, also transactions that were connected to ethnic cleansing[317].

Until the Law on Cessation in 1998, the CRPC remained the main defender of restitution rights in a time where local authorities did not invest their efforts to engage in property restitution. Towards the end of its mandate in 2003, it was able to proceed 240,333 claims for 319,220 properties, in cooperation with municipalities who carried out the work actual work[318]. The Office of the High Representative recognised in 1999, that without enforcement, the decisions made by the CRPC would have very little effect. In the "Decision of the Recognition and Implementation of CRPC Decision in the Federation", Article 2, says that all decisions made by CRPC are "final and binding from the day of their adoption", making it domestic law[319].

In order to centralise the work on property claims, the Office of the High Representative (OHR), the Office of the UNCHR, the Organisation for Security and Cooperation in Europe (OSCE) and the UN Mission in Bosnia and Hercegovina (UNMBIH), 'joined forces' and created the Property Law Implementation Plan (PLIP) in 1999. UNCHR acting under Annex 7 of the General Framework Agreement for

---

[314] Philpott, see page 42.
[315] GFA; Annex 7, Chapter Two, Article VII.
[316] Ibid, see Article IX.
[317] GFA, Annex 7, Chapter Two, Article XII (3) "In determining the lawful owner of any property, the Commission shall not recognize as valid any illegal property transaction, including any transfer that was made under duress, in exchange for exit permission or documents, or that was otherwise in connection with ethnic cleansing. Any person who is awarded return of property may accept a satisfactory lease arrangement rather than retake possession".
[318] Philpott, see page 40.
[319] OHR, "Decision on the Recognition and Implementation of CRPC Decisions in the Federation" at http://www.ohr.int/?p=67636 (27.10.1999), Article 2, available at and "Decision on the recognition and Implementation of CRPC Decisions in the RS", Article 2, (27.10.1999) available at http://www.ohr.int/?p=67632 (Viewed at 13.08.16).

Peace recognised that property restitution was a precondition to return. CRPC, acknowledged that without the support of the local authority it would be difficult to solve disputes. Organisations under the mandate of Annex 6, such as the OSCE, ensured that the European Convention on Human Rights Article 8 and Article 1 of the First Protocol were satisfied[320].

The implementation plan created a monitoring scheme, in which CRPC had observer status. A monitoring officer was placed in every municipality to ensure that implementation took place, it was also focused on creating a good working relationship with the police to ensure enforcement. The Focal Point Scheme was central in monitoring activities and a linkage between local authorities and international organisations[321].

In December 2001, the Office of the High Representative issued 13 decisions in regard to further regulation of property restitution, transparency and deadlines[322]. One decision that stands out, was the decision to review application in the order it was received[323]. The restitution laws set a thirty-day deadline, from the day a claim was filed to the time a decision was made. It is worth bearing in mind, that most applications were filled in from 1998-2000, and that the capacity for reviewing them took more than one month; however, prioritising the claims and following the principle 'First come, first served' made the process go much more 'smoother'[324].

By early 2004, about one-third of all property claims in all Bosnian municipalities with significant property claims caseload, had been verified. Most of the municipalities were in their final stage of completing property restitution claims. The Office of the High Representative, the United Nations High Commissioner for Refugees and the OSCE Mission to Bosnia and Hercegovina stated in December, that the property law implementation plan ratio had reached 92.5 %. Local housing authorities had finalized 201,902 of total 281,310 property claims registered[325].

---

[320] Philpott, see page 43.

[321] OSCE Mission to Bosnia and Hercegovina, Property Law Implementation Plan (PLIP), Inter – Agency Framework Document (15.10.2000), available at http://www.ohr.int/?ohr_archive=plip-inter-agency-framework-document (Viewed at 13.08.16).

[322] All 13 decisions can be found available at http://www.ohr.int/?month=12&year=2001&page_id=1196 (Viewed at 13.08.16).

[323] OHR, "Decision Enacting the law on amendments to the Law on the Cessation of Application of the Law on Temporary Abandoned Real Property Owned by Citizens (FBiH)" (4.12.2001), see Article 5, available at http://www.ohr.int/?p=66920 and "Decision Enacting The Law On Amendments To The Law On The Cessation Of Application Of The Law On The Use Of Abandoned Property (RS)", (4.12.2001), see Article 7, available at http://www.ohr.int/?p=66889 (Viewed at 13.08.16).

[324] Philpott, page 56.

It is worth noting, that the right to return is just a right, as it is not an obligation for refugees or internally displaced to return home. Charles B. Philpott argues, that it is simply a duty for the parties to the General Framework Agreement for Peace; Republika Srpska and the Federation of Bosnia and Hercegovina, to create the conditions for those who wish to return[326]. However, Annex 6 of the Agreement, "The Agreement on Human Rights", makes the European Convention on Human Rights applicable to all Bosnian jurisdictions. This includes right to "respect home" under Article 8[327] and the right "to property" under Article 1 of the First Protocol[328].

Any violation to the European Convention on Human Rights, could be reviewed by the human rights institutions established under Annex 6 of the General Framework Agreement for Peace. This includes the CRPC, the Ombudsman, and the High Representative. Cases have also been brought before the European Court of Human Rights, especially civil actions under the ordinary rules of tort law. One case that stands out is Đokić v. Bosnia and Herzegovina. The case concerned the applicant's impossibility to regain possession of a flat he wished to re-register in his name, which he had bought and left in Sarajevo during the war 1992-1995. The court held that Đokić was treated differently (he was a Serb), even if the applicable law seemed neutral, and the composition offered was too low[329].

In reaching the decision regarding Đokić, the court recognised many of the challenges in connection to the property restitution process in Bosnia and Hercegovina. One challenge relates to remedies for individual violations, another challenge is connected to the compensation for possessions and property. Importantly, the court recognised that the legal ground for property restitution for refugees and internally displaced is two-fold[330],: in referring to the Pinheiro

---

[325] OHR, Property Law implementation in Bosnia and Herzegovina nears completion", Press Release (11.2.2004), http://www.ohr.int/?p=46599 (Viewed at 13.08.16).

[326] Philpott, see page 37.

[327] European Convention on Human Rights (ECHR): Article 8 (1), "Everyone has the right to respect for his private and family life, his home and his correspondence."

[328] See ECHR, First Protocol to the Convention for Protection of Human Rights and Fundamental Freedoms: Article 1 "Every natural or legal person is entitled to the peaceful enjoyment of his possessions. No one shall be deprived of his possessions except in the public interest and subject to the conditions provided for by law and by the general principles of international law. The preceding provisions shall not, however, in any way impair the right of a State to enforce such laws as it deems necessary to control the use of property in accordance with the general interest or to secure the payment of taxes or other contributions or penalties".

[329] Đokić v. Bosnia and Hercegovina [04/10/2010] ECHR Application no. 6518/04 See para 60.

[330] Ibid, see para 50.

Principles, adopted by the UN Sub-Commission on the Promotion and Protection of Human Rights in 2005, the court referred to one right in relation to return and the other right is in relation to compensation[331].

While the restitution process remains at an early stage of UN adoption, they clearly detect that restitution is viewed as pertinent in the context of displacement and return[332], this perspective was shaped by the experience in Bosnia and Hercegovina. The implementation process focused specifically on two factors: first, Annex 7 of the General Framework Agreement connected the right to return with restitution; second, the right to restitution facilitated significant return movement. The reparation measures prescribed in the peace treaty focused heavily on the return aspect rather than the actually reparative measures[333]. Even though Annex 7 specifically says "refugees and internally displaces shall.... be compensated for any property that cannot be restored to them"[334], a fund to deal with compensation was never set up by the international community[335]. International Centre for Transitional Justice (ICJT) concluded in 2004 that no comprehensive reparation programme existed in Bosnia[336].

Outstanding war-damage payments remain quite challenging in Bosnia and Hercegovina. Until 2003, cases on war-damages, were reviewed by the CRPC or brought before the Human Rights Chamber for Bosnia and Hercegovina (re-named to Human Rights Commission, which is a part of the Bosnian constitutional court). The Human Rights Commission only reviews cases registered with the Chamber before 31. December 2003[337]. 12 individual compensation claims have been brought forward; 7 cases were registered in 1998, 4 in 1999 and 1 in 2002[338].

---

[331] Commission on Human Rights, Sub-Commission on the Promotion and Protection of Human Rights, "Housing and property restitution in the context of the return of refugees and internally displaced persons", E/CN.4/Sub.2/2005/17 (28.June 2005), available at http://unispal.un.org/UNISPAL.NSF/0/577D69B243FD3C0485257075006698E6 (Viewed 13.08.16).

[332] Report of the Secretary-General, "The rule of law and transitional justice in conflict and post-conflict societies" (23.August 2004) UNSC S/2004/616, at http://www.ipu.org/splz-e/unga07/law.pdf see para 54.

[333] Eric Rosand, The Right to Compensation in Bosnia: An Unfulfilled Promise and Challenge to International Law, Cornell International Law Journal, Vol. 33, Issue 1 (2000), 113-157, see page 114-115.

[334] GFA, Annex 7, Article 1(1).

[335] Rosand, see page 131.

[336] International Center for Transitional Justice, Bosnia and Hercegovina: selected developments in transitional justice, (2004), available at
https://www.ictj.org/sites/default/files/ICTJ-FormerYugoslavia-Bosnia-Developments-2004-English.pdf
See page 11.

[337] Bosnian Human Rights Commission, "Introduction", available at

After 2003, claims in regard to war-damage property, were mainly left with the local courts, the Prosecutor's Office a Special Department for War Crimes, and other instances established under Annex 6 of the General Framework Agreement for Peace. According to Criminal Procedure Code of Bosnia and Hercegovina, a property claim may be related to pecuniary or non-pecuniary damages resulting from a criminal offense.[339] However, claims for compensations are not resolved in criminal verdicts, the court of Bosnia and Hercegovina refers the injured party to file a civil lawsuit, which many victims cannot initiate due to lack of financial means. Cases on property damage are long, complex[340], and to date, no compensation has been issued[341].

A leading judgement concerning the non-enforcement of domestic courts decisions ordering payment was made by the ECHR in 2009 in the case Čolić and Others v. Bosnia and Herzegovina. The court it its judgment, urged the state of Bosnia and Hercegovina to make the necessary payments within three months[342]. The ECHR found also that the judgements made by Human Rights Commission in Bosnia and Hercegovina, were not enforced by the parties involved[343]. Even if one does not accept state responsibility, the court in its judgement, emphasised the responsibility the Government of Bosnia and Hercegovina has[344]. Based of Annex 7 General Framework Agreement for Peace, the Government (both entities) are obliged to find the funding necessary in order to pay compensation, as all parties agreed to this when they signed the peace treaty.

Destruction of homes and properties was a tool of ethnic cleansing during the conflict in Bosnia and Hercegovina; confiscation of property and razing of homes

---

http://www.hrc.ba/commission/eng/default.htm (Viewed at 13.08.16).
[338] Ibid, "Decisions" http://www.hrc.ba/commission/eng/decisions/results.asp (Viewed at 13.08.16).
[339] Criminal Procedure Code of Bosnia and Hercegovina, 'Official Gazette' of Bosnia and Hercegovina" Official Gazette of Bosnia and Herzegovina, No. 3/03, 32/03, 36/03, 26/04, 63/04, 13/05, 48/05, 46/06, 76/06, 29/07, 32/07, 53/07, 76/07,15/08, 58/08, 12/09, 16/09, 93/09.
[340] Selma Ucanbarlic, "No Compensation for War Crime Victims", for Balkan Insight (28. November 2011), available at http://www.balkaninsight.com/en/article/no-compensation-for-war-crime-victims (Viewed at 13.08.16).
[341] Denis Dzidic "Bosnian War Victims Still Awaiting for Compensation" for Balkan Transitional Justice (01. April 2015), available at http://www.balkaninsight.com/en/article/bosnian-war-victims-still-waiting-for-compensation (Viewed at 13.08.16).
[342] Čolić and Others v. Bosnia and Herzegovina [28.06.2010] Applications nos. 1218/07, 1240/07, 1242/07, 1335/07, 1368/07, 1369/07, 3424/07, 3428/07, 3430/07, 3935/07, 3940/07, 7194/07, 7204/07, 7206/07 and 7211/07
[343] Ibid, see para 8 and 9.
[344] Rosand, see 146-147.

and farms to the ground was carried out to preclude the possibility of return. The violent circumstances forced people to leave their homes and belongings behind. As local authorities approved of this practice, the responsibility to pay compensation would therefore fall back on the Government of Bosnia and Hercegovina[345].

Eric Rosand argues that the right to compensation might have a negative impact on long-term peace and stability in Bosnia and Hercegovina. The failure to implement the right compensation has left those who do not wish to return without redress for the property violations that occurred during and after the war. Rosand continues to argue that it would be wrong to address compensation issues for people living in Bosnia and Hercegovina without taking into account refugees who have chosen not return[346].

## The Rule Of Law In Peacebuilding

To avoid 'politicized' approach of property restitution rights, the international community began empathizing the 'rule of law' approach in 2000, stressing that all claims should be addressed by local authorities, regardless of whether claimants intended to return or not. The objective was to establish equal opportunities for all the three ethnical groups. The focus on rule of law was affirmed by PLIP monitoring group in March 2000[347].

Peacebuilding involves a wide range of different measures targeted to create long-term peace and development. One strategy to prevent a society to relapse into conflict, is strengthening the concept of the rule of law in peacebuilding. Conflict tends to breakdown rule of law, and rebuilding and strengthen the rule of law tends to be complex and challenging. Even though each conflict is different, challenges connected to the rule of law tends to be similar; lack of material and human capacity and lack of trust to the existing the rule of law institutions. Weakness in these institutions and laws, have often caused conflicts and present a threat to independence, impartiality and effectiveness to institutions in the aftermath of a conflict[348].

The UN Secretary-General in a report in 2004, addressed the importance of incorporating rule of law in peacebuilding based on the experience, that peace in the long-run, cannot be achieved unless the population is confident that redress for grievances can be achieved through legitimate structures for peaceful settlements

---

[345] Ibid, pp. 118-119.
[346] Ibid, pp. 132-133.
[347] Williams, p. 524.
[348] United Nations Peacekeeping "Rule of Law", available at http://www.un.org/en/peacekeeping/issues/ruleoflaw.shtml (Viewed at 13.08.16).

and fair administration of justice[349]. The Secretary-General defined rule of law as following:

> "It refers to a principle of governance in which all persons, institutions and entities, public and private, including the State itself, are accountable to laws that are publicly promulgated, equally enforced and independently adjudicated, and which are consistent with international human rights norms and standards. It requires, as well, measures to ensure adherence to the principles of supremacy of law, equality before the law, accountability to the law, fairness in the application of the law, separation of powers, participation in decision-making, legal certainty, avoidance of arbitrariness and procedural and legal transparency"[350].

How to strengthen rule of law, depends more or less, how one views rule of law and what goals one is trying to achieve through rule of law. Rachel Kleinfeld Belton argues two perspectives in this regard. The first perspective deals with which ends, rule of law intends to serve within a society (upholding the rule of law, providing efficient judgement). Belton continues to argue, that the ends-based perspective serves not only one common good, but five, 'ends goods':

1. Government bound by law;
2. Equality before the law;
3. Law and order;
4. Predictable and effective rulings;
5. Lack of human rights violations.

The other perspective focuses on how institutional attributes can contribute to the rule of law (well-functioning courts, trained law enforcement agencies)[351]. The definition by the Secretary-General can be argued from the first perspective, the ends based, as nature law is also taken into consideration; however, can the Bosnian restitution process be viewed from this perspective?

Access to land and the ability to use it, is an effective factor in reducing poverty and in creating economic prosper. This is also why ownership and individual rights to land, is of importance in post- conflict societies. In the case of Bosnia, it was viewed as a central element in peacebuilding, in solving disputes. Rhodri C. Williams

---

[349] Report of the Secretary-General.
[350] Ibid, see para 6.
[351] Rachel Kleinfeld Belton, Competing definitions of the rule of law: implications for practitioners, Carnegie Papers, Rule of Law Series, No.55 (Carnegie Endowment for International Peace), see page 3 and 5-15.

worked as an officer for OSCE during the time of property restitution in Bosnia and has written and published books and academic papers on the process[352]. Regarding the restitution process, he says as following:

> "A central lesson of Bosnian restitution is that adoption of a rights-based approach at the outset of restitution processes is more likely to ensure property repossession in a fair, efficient, and transparent manner for all victims of displacement. This, in turn, will facilitate informed choices by each restitution beneficiary on whether to return to their original home or use it as an asset to fund sustainable resettlement elsewhere"[353].

The rights-based approach focused, on occupancy rights and protecting those rights from "secondary occupants" who came to reside on property, which did not belong to them. Interpretations from PLIP, recognized the need to break down the formal link between apartment repossessions and return. This was recognised as a necessary measure from the international community, in order to encourage refugees and internally displaced to return 'home'. The focus was on creating an environment in which people voluntarily wanted to go home, even if the case was to sell their home and resettle somewhere else. The rights – based approach provided choices, choices for the refugees and internally displaced to make on their own, regardless of regime or political influence[354].

The enforcement of this policy came from several holds. One implementation mechanism came from UNMIBH, which issued a ruling in regard to the police. Those who wished to remain in their positions should vacate property belonging to others. Another implementation mechanism was to create a rule, to remove local authorities residing illegally[355].

In regards to the rule of law requirements, one can argue that the Bosnian restitution process fulfilled the criteria's. It practiced equality before the law, it was fair in the application process, it participated in the decision-making, it removed any obstacles, it resolved challenges fairly and the entire process was transparent. Importantly, all of the people in Bosnia and Hercegovina, accepted the process as all were treated in the same way, neither group was favoured and all claims were processed equally. However, the strong presence of the international community and the Bonn powers admitted to the High Representative, guaranteed that the housing

---

[352] Williams, see page 441 footnotes.
[353] Ibid.
[354] Ibid, pp 519-520.
[355] Philpott, pp. 59-60.

restitution process went according to plan. The weak state institutions of Bosnia and Hercegovina would not have been able to provide for equal rights[356].

## How Can The Bosnian Experience Be Applicable In Other Post-Conflict Societies?

Despite this controversy, Bosnia has become the leading model for achieving post-conflict restitution as *per se* right and a tool in promoting refugee return. Since the conflict ended in 1995, Bosnia has been held up as a model in solving property disputes from NGO's to UN Special Rapporteurs[357], in areas such as Palestine[358] and Iraq (after 2003)[359]. However, examining post-conflict societies and countries where Bosnia has been recognised as the leading model, reveal the same uneasy questions regarding the relationship between restitution and refugees. How each post-conflict society has dealt with this particular issue has varied – as the legal source and the justification to rights have been and are different[360].

However, there are three main lessons we draw from the Bosnian experience, which can be applicable to other post-societies in regard to property restitution and disputes of land.

The first lesson learned, is the length of displacement, which was relatively short compared to other post-conflict societies. According to statistics kept by UNCHR Representation in Bosnia and Hercegovina, 987,713 refugees and internally displaced persons had returned to their pre-war homes by December 2003[361]. The length of displacement helped sort out the 'occupancy' rights. The longer the displacement is the more challenging it gets starting property restitution. This was the case in Rwanda after the genocide in 1994, which also dealt with displacement of refugees from the conflict in 1959, known as the "1959 refugees" and "old caseloads". In the end of 1994, refugees were returning to Rwanda uncontrolled. International agencies had fled the country before the genocide and did not return immediately. It also took

---

[356] Katayanagi, p. 16.

[357] Williams, p 446.

[358] Paul Prettitore, Why Not Palestine?, available at http://www.badil.org/en/publication/periodicals/al-majdal/item/989-why-not-palestine?.html (Viewed at 13.08.16).

[359] U.S Institute of Peace, Avoiding Violence in Kirkuk Requires Settling Property Disputes Quickly (April 28, 2003) available at http://www.usip.org/publications/avoiding-violence-in-kirkuk-requires-settling-property-disputes-quickly (Viewed at 13.08.16).

[360] Williams, p.447.

[361] Fernando del Mundo for UNCHR, "UN refugee agency report 1,415 returns in Bosnia and Hercegovina in February" (13. April 2004), available at http://www.unhcr.org/407bf7cd4.html (Viewed at 13.08.16).

time for the new government to begin its work. The lack of structure and enforcement led to refugees residing on property not belonging to them[362]. One remaining challenge, is that many Rwandan refugees are still located in the neighbouring countries such as Tanzania and Uganda. Another challenge is that Rwanda has become a residing country for refugees from other countries, mainly from the Democratic Republic of Congo[363].

The second lesson, we can draw from the Bosnian experience, is the strong presence of the international community after the conflict ended in 1995. By the end of 1996, about 200 non-governmental (NGO), 27 intergovernmental organisations, 18 UN agencies, and 17 different foreign government, were involved in reconstruction efforts. It has been calculated that Bosnian inhabitants, have received more aid per capita, than any other European countries after the Second World War. Much of the funding comes from the World Bank and the European Union[364].

The High Representative represents the international community's commitments and presence in Bosnia and Hercegovina. Without the powers granted him, and the strong focus on enforcing mechanisms, the restitution process, would probably have been blocked by ethno-politics. Importantly, the Bosnian leadership did not challenge the legitimacy of the High Representative, as everyone were treated equally[365]. This support enhanced the restitution process; securing the rights for all involved, ensuring that all are neutral before the law, remains challenging in ethnical divided countries; Kosovo is an example of that. The Organisation for Security and Cooperation in Europe (OSCE) reported that local judges in Kosovo fail to maintain neutral in some cases. This is the case in Mitrovica (Municipality in Kosovo – at the border to Serbia), where the problem of dual sovereignty between Kosovo and Serbia, remain an issue[366]. Many property restitution claims are often

---

[362] John W. Bruce, Return of land in post-conflict Rwanda: International standards, improvisation, and the role of international humanitarian organizations, in *Land and Post-Conflict Peacebuilding*, (ed.) Jon Unruh and Rhodri C. Williams (London: Earthscan, 2013), 121-144, see pages 125-126.
[363] UNCHR, "Rwanda – 2015 UNCHR country operations profile", available at http://www.unhcr.org/rwanda.html (Viewed at 13.08.16).
[364] Lana Pasic, Bosnia's Vast Foreign Financial Assistance Re-Examined: Statistics and Results at Balkan Anaysis, available at
http://www.balkanalysis.com/bosnia/2011/06/21/bosnia%e2%80%99s-vast-foreign-financial-assistance-re-examined-statistics-and-results/ (Viewed at 13.08.16).
[365] Rhodri C. Williams, Post-conflict land tenure issues in Bosnia: Privatization and the politics of reintegrating the displaced in *Land and Post-Conflict Peacebuilding*, (ed.) Jon Unruh and Rhodri C. Williams (London: Earthscan, 2013), pp. 145-175, see pages 167-168.
[366] OSCE Mission to Kosovo, "Challenges in the Resolution of Conflict-Related Property Claims in Kosovo" Report, June 2011, available at

refereed to local courts, which lack both human and financial resources to review them[367].

CRPC was the institution in Bosnia and Hercegovina, which handled property claims. It was not an international institution; however, the composition of members included also representatives from the international community and it was internationally funded. Its composition secured neutrality, which on-blocked ethno-politics and provided assistance to property owners. On the role CRPC played, Charles Philpott says, "it was the main defender of restitution rights at a time when the domestic authorities were intent upon consolidating and legalising post factum the wartime ethnic-cleansing"[368].

The third lesson, the Bosnian experience can teach us, is the focus on property rights and ownership. The challenge in Bosnia and Hercegovina was not establishing ownership nor getting hold of property documentation; merely establishing 'occupancy' rights. In many developing countries, registration and documentation remain 'road blocks' in solving questions of land. Most land in Sub-Saharan Africa have no registration of who owns it or has the rights to use it. The reasons for this are multiple and overlapping; first rights, conquer rights, allocation by local and national government, long occupation and use, and market transaction, are some reasons. Property restitution in some of these countries, require a series of overlapping claims, dependent on customary use, season and negotiations[369]. Some governments are reluctant to transfer full property rights to their citizens. In Tanzania, the president holds all the rights to land "in the name of the citizens[370]".

## Conclusion

Reviewing the Bosnian experience in regard to property restitution, makes us believe that the Bosnian model can easily be applied to other post-conflict societies. However, examples mentioned above, illustrates the complexity in solving land disputes around the world. Every case is different, as its history and justification to rights, are different. The reasons for solving disputes of land are also different. In Bosnia and Hercegovina, property restitution was viewed as a measure to rebuild a society after conflict and build bridges between the three ethnical groups. While the

---

http://www.osce.org/kosovo/80435?download=true, see page 9.

[367] Ibid, p. 8.

[368] Philpott, p. 40.

[369] Camilla Toulmin, Securing land and property rights in sub-Saharan Africa: the role of local institutions in Securing Land and Property Rights: Improving the Investment Climate Global Competiveness, Report 2005-06 World Economic Forum, 27-54, see page 32-33.

[370] Ibid, p. 38.

property restitution has been successful in Bosnia and Hercegovina, the international community's efforts in creating a functioning multi-ethnic state, failed. The international community have not been able to transfer the rule of law experience from property restitution, to other parts of the society. Even though, the Dayton agreement was successful in ending the bloodshed in the country, it laid the framework for a dysfunctional and instable state. The conflict from 1992-1995, created three ethnical lines, lines which the peace treaty recognised in its diving of the country, lines which the people of Bosnia and Hercegovina still live by and the legacy of war still burdens the Bosnian society. However, the Bosnian experience is solving disputes of land, stands out in the discussion of land rights; the Bosnian model in itself provides knowledge and lessons that can lead to solid peacebuilding.

# References

Bosnian Human Rights Commission, "Introduction", available at http://www.hrc.ba/commission/eng/default.htm

Bosnian Human Rights Commission, "Decisions", available at http://www.hrc.ba/commission/eng/decisions/results.asp

Bosnian Ministry of Human Rights and Refugees, Comparative Analysis on Access to Right to Refugees and Displaced Persons (September 2005), available at http://www.mhrr.gov.ba/PDF/default.aspx?id=283&langTag=bs-BA

Camilla Toulmin, Securing land and property rights in sub-Saharan Africa: the role of local institutions in Securing Land and Property Rights: Improving the Investment Climate Global Competiveness, Report 2005-06 World Economic Forum, 27-54.

Case No. CH/98/659: Pletili´c and others. against Republika Srpska, Decision on Request for Review, Human Rights Chamber in Bosnia and Hercegovina (September 10, 1999), available at http://www.hrc.ba/database/decisions/CH98-659%20et%20al%20Pletilic%20et%20al%20Request%20for%20review%20E.pdf

Charles B. Philpott, From the Right to Return to the Return of Rights: Complementing Post-War Property Restitution in Bosnia and Hercegovina, International Journal of Refugee Law, Vol. 18 No.1 (2006).

Commission on Human Rights, Sub-Commission on the Promotion and Protection of Human Rights, "Housing and property restitution in the context of the return of refugees and internally displaced persons", E/CN.4/Sub.2/2005/17 (28.June 2005), available at https://unispal.un.org/DPA/DPR/unispal.nsf/0/577D69B243FD3C0485257075006698 E6

Criminal Procedure Code of Bosnia and Hercegovina, 'Official Gazette' of Bosnia and Hercegovina" Official Gazette of Bosnia and Herzegovina, No. 3/03, 32/03, 36/03, 26/04, 63/04, 13/05, 48/05, 46/06, 76/06, 29/07, 32/07, 53/07, 76/07,15/08, 58/08, 12/09, 16/09, 93/09.

Čolić and Others v. Bosnia and Herzegovina [28.06.2010] Applications nos. 1218/07, 1240/07, 1242/07, 1335/07, 1368/07, 1369/07, 3424/07, 3428/07, 3430/07, 3935/07, 3940/07, 7194/07, 7204/07, 7206/07 and 7211/07.

Denis Dzidic "Bosnian War Victims Still Awaiting for Compensation" for Balkan Transitional Justice (01. April 2015), available at http://www.balkaninsight.com/en/article/bosnian-war-victims-still-waiting-for-compensation

Đokić v. Bosnia and Hercegovina [04/10/2010] ECHR Application no. 6518/04.

Eric Rosand, The Right to Compensation in Bosnia: An Unfulfilled Promise and Challenge to International Law, Cornell International Law Journal, Vol. 33, Issue 1 (2000), 113-157.

European Convention on Human Rights.

FBH Official Gazette, no. 11/98.

Fernando del Mundo for UNCHR, "UN refugee agency report 1,415 returns in Bosnia and Hercegovina in February" (13. April 2004), available at http://www.unhcr.org/407bf7cd4.html

International Covenant for Civil and Political Rights

International Covenant for Economic, Social and Cultural Rights

International Center for Transitional Justice, Bosnia and Hercegovina: selected developments in transitional justice, (2004), available at https://www.ictj.org/sites/default/files/ICTJ-FormerYugoslavia-Bosnia-Developments-2004-English.pdf

Lana Pasic, Bosnia's Vast Foreign Financial Assistance Re-Examined: Statistics and Results at Balkan Anaysis, available at http://www.balkanalysis.com/bosnia/2011/06/21/bosnia%e2%80%99s-vast-foreign-financial-assistance-re-examined-statistics-and-results/

Law on Use of Abandoned Property, Official Gazette of the Republika Srpska, Nos. 3/96, 21/96. See also The institution of Human Rights Ombudsman in Bosnia and Hercegovina, Special Report of the Ombudsman in BiH dealing with abandoned property in BiH, 24 May 2012, available at http://www.ombudsmen.gov.ba/documents/obmudsmen_doc2013020406405420eng.pdf

John W. Bruce, Return of land in post-conflict Rwanda: International standards, improvisation, and the role of international humanitarian organizations, in Land and Post-Conflict Peacebuilding, (ed.) Jon Unruh and Rhodri C. Williams (London: Earthscan, 2013), pp. 121-144.

Mari Katayanagi, Property Restitution and the Rule of Law in Peacebuilding: Examining the Applicability of the Bosnian model, Paper prepared for presentation at the 2014 World Bank Conference On Land And Poverty The World Bank - Washington DC, March 24-27, 2014.

Office of the High Representative, "General Information" available at http://www.ohr.int/?page_id=1139

Office of the High Representative, "Cessation of the Application of the Law on the Use of Abandoned Property", (27.10.1999).

Office of the High Representative, "Decision on the Recognition and Implementation of CRPC Decisions in the Federation" (27.10.1999).

Office of the High Representative, "Decision on the recognition and Implementation of CRPC Decisions in the RS", (27.10.1999).

Office of the High Representative, "Decision Enacting the law on amendments to the Law on the Cessation of Application of the Law on Temporary Abandoned Real Property Owned by Citizens (FBiH), (4.12.2001).

Office of the High Representative, "Decision Enacting The Law On Amendments To The Law On The Cessation Of Application Of The Law On The Use Of Abandoned Property (RS)", (4.12.2001).

Office of the High Representative, "Property Law implementation in Bosnia and Hercegovina nears completion", Press Release (11.2.2004).

Office of the High Representative, "Decision on the Instruction on Application of the Law on Cessation of Application of the Law on Abandoned Apartments in its amended form", (16.05.2003).

OSCE Mission to Bosnia and Hercegovina, Property Law Implementation Plan (PLIP), Inter – Agency Framework Document (15.10.2000).

OSCE Mission to Kosovo, "Challenges in the Resolution of Conflict-Related Property Claims in Kosovo" Report, June 2011, available at http://www.osce.org/kosovo/80435?download=true,

Paul Prettitore, Why Not Palestine?, available at http://www.badil.org/en/publication/periodicals/al-majdal/item/989-why-not-palestine?.html

Rachel Kleinfeld Belton, Competing definitions of the rule of law: implications for practitioners, Carnegie Papers, Rule of Law Series, No.55 (Carnegie Endowment for International Peace).

Report of the Secretary-General, "The rule of law and transitional justice in conflict and post-conflict societies" (23.August 2004) UNSC S/2004/616.

Rhodri C. Williams, Post-Conflict Property Restitution and Refugee Return in Bosnia and Hercegovina: Implications for International Standard-Setting and Practice, New York University Journal of International Law and Politics, Vol. 37 No.3 (2005), 441-553.

Rhodri C. Williams, Post-conflict land tenure issues in Bosnia: Privatization and the politics of reintegrating the displaced in Land and Post-Conflict Peacebuilding , (ed.) Jon Unruh and Rhodri C. Williams (London: Earthscan, 2013), pp. 145-175.

RS Official Gazette, no. 38/98.

Selma Ucanbarlic, "No Compensation for War Crime Victims", for Balkan Insight (28. November 2011), available at http://www.balkaninsight.com/en/article/no-compensation-for-war-crime-victims

The General Framework for Peace.

UN Declaration on Human Rights.

UNCHR, "Rwanda – 2015 UNCHR country operations profile", available at http://www.unhcr.org/rwanda.html

UN-Habitat, Housing and Property Rights in Bosnia and Hercegovina, Croatia and Serbia and Montenegro (2005) can be found available at file:///C:/Users/Bruker/Downloads/2130_alt.pdf

UNSC resolution 1031 (1995).

UNSC resolution 1031

United Nations Peacekeeping "Rule of Law", available at http://www.un.org/en/peacekeeping/issues/ruleoflaw.shtml

U.S Institute of Peace, Avoiding Violence in Kirkuk Requires Settling Property Disputes Quickly (April 28, 2003) available at http://www.usip.org/publications/avoiding-violence-in-kirkuk-requires-settling-property-disputes-quickly

1951 Convention Relating to the Status of Refugees

# The Securitisation Of The UK

Refugees perceived as potential terrorists and their resulting treatment within the international legal framework by the UK

## Robert W. Reed

*Recent history has been marked by a number of forced migrations as a result of wars, famine, or socio-economic factors which provide significant push and pull factors for migrants to travel to the EU. A narrative persists that these migrants contain an element which includes a number of terrorists, or those who may have committed serious criminal acts; furthermore, this narrative espouses the idea the idea that these persons secreted among the migrants are both unable to be refused the status of refugee protection, and that the state is impotent to remove these persons from the EU, and particularly the UK. This paper will explore these narratives and juxtapose them with the appropriate legislation and case law; finally, this paper will explore possible solutions to the 'migrant crisis' based on the concerns expressed by states and their citizens.*

## Introduction

This work will seek to explain and critique the nexus, in practice, between the areas of International Refugee Law, Extradition Law, International Human Rights Law, International Humanitarian Law, and International Criminal Law: Articles 1F, and 32 & 33 of the United Nations Convention relating to the Status of Refugees of 1951 and the amended protocol of 1967, and how a limited number of the commensurate British legal framework measures are used in order to firstly, protect the security of British citizens, and secondly, uphold the obligations of the UK under the requisite international treaties.

This work will be mindful of the Othman v UK case as an example of the situation which is often cited as an example of why the UK should remove itself from the jurisdiction of the European Court of Human Rights (ECtHR)[371].

Pertinent to this discussion, are the *obiter* remarks of Lord Brown in JS v UK, "that there can only be one true interpretation of article 1F(a), an autonomous meaning to be found in international rather than domestic law...[and] that the international instruments referred to in the article are those existing when disqualification is being considered, not merely those extant at the date of the Convention... [Furthermore,] that because of the serious consequences of exclusion for the person concerned the article must be interpreted restrictively and used cautiously"[372]. While all of the international instruments have their domestic equivalent, or at least transpose them in to UK legislation, their lordships' approach is prudent, as many of the domestically distilled provisions were never envisioned to be enacted in such a manner by the drafters[373].

Discussion of particular sub-section crimes pursuant to Art 1F, such as Art 1F(a) - grave breaches of the Geneva convention - are beyond the scope of this work due to its length, and the paper will merely attempt to address the issue of what measures are open to the UK in order to take action against those who would subject to those Art 1F instruments, from a generalist point of view. The paper will also concentrate solely non-UK citizen members of groups such as Islamic State, and those that might have well been involved in acts of terror to a minor degree whom might seek refuge within the United Kingdom to avoid the possibility of prosecution in addition to any refugee claim that they might have.

This work does not address the relative merits of the refugee system in regard to migrants seeking refugee protection in general, some of which have been identified as being manifestly unfair, and prevent access to redress of decisions[374], although

---

[371] Travis A, 'Theresa May Criticises Human Rights Convention after Abu Qatada Affair' (2013) <http://www.theguardian.com/world/2013/jul/08/theresa-may-human-rights-abu-qatada> accessed 23/04/2015

[372] *R (on the Application of Js) (Sri Lanka) (Respondent) V Secretary of State for the Home Department (Appellant)* United Kingdom Supreme Court Reports (Supreme Court)

[373] Feller E, Turk V and Nicholson F, 'Refugee Protection in International Law' (2003) UNHCR's Global Consultations on International Protection

[374] ECRE, ECRE Comments on Regulation (EU) No 604/2013 of the European Parliament and of the Council of 26 June 2013 Establishing the Criteria and Mechanisms for Determining the Member State Responsible for Examining an Application for International Protection Lodged in One of the Member States by a Third-Country National or a Stateless Person (Recast). 2015); UNHCR, Un High Commissioner for Refugees (UNHCR), Unhcr Comments on the European Commission's Proposal for a Recast of the Regulation of the European Parliament and of the Council Establishing the Criteria and Mechanisms for Determining the Member State Responsible for Examining an Application for International Protection Lodged in One of the Member States by a Third Country National or a Stateless Person ("Dublin II") (Com(2008) 820, 3 December 2008) and the European

these systems will be discussed in regard to their ability to fulfil the core discussion of their ability to add to the security of the UK within an international refugee law context.

## Articles Of Definition And Protection

The United Nations Convention relating to the Status of Refugees of 1951 and the amended protocol of 1967 (CSR) gives the definition of a 'refugee'[375] within Art 1A:

> "owing to well-founded fear of being persecuted for reasons of race, religion, nationality, membership of a particular social group or political opinion, is outside the country of his nationality and is unable or, owing to such fear, is unwilling to avail himself of the protection of that country; or who, not having a nationality and being outside the country of his former habitual residence, is unable or, owing to such fear, is unwilling to return to it."

Furthermore, Arts 32 & 33(1) give the protections which are owed by a state to a *de jure* refugee, that they should not suffer refoulement, without due process.

Art 33(1) prevents the refoulement of persons whose life, or freedom, would be threatened by their return to the frontiers of any territory which would do so on the basis of their race, religion, nationality, membership of a particular social group, or political opinion. Critics of the system would point to Art 33(1), or the ECHR Art 3, and how these seemingly conspire to prevent the expulsion of people who have come to the UK for protection, and then wish to upset the established way of life within the UK[376].

Aside the CSR and the ECHR, there are two other international conventions which the UK is a party to which would provide protection from refoulement to states who may torture, the 1984 Convention against Torture and Other Cruel, Inhuman or Degrading Treatment or Punishment (CAT); and, 1966 International Covenant on Civil and Political Rights (ICCPR).

---

Commission's Proposal for a Recast of the Regulation of the European Parliament and of the Council Concerning the Establishment of 'Eurodac' for the Comparison of Fingerprints for the Effective Application of [the Dublin Ii Regulation] (Com(2008) 825, 3 December 2008), 2009)

[375] The 1951 Convention Relating to the Status of Refugees and the 1967 Protocol

[376] Editorial, 'Abu Qatada Awarded Compensation by European Judges for 'Breach of Human Rights'' (*Telegraph*, 2009) <http://www.telegraph.co.uk/news/uknews/4696480/Abu-Qatada-awarded-compensation-by-European-judges-for-breach-of-human-rights.html> accessed 9 December 2014

Under CAT, the principle of Non-refoulement is limited to de facto torture only, it does not extend to less serious treatment under Art 3 of this convention; unlike the ECHR Art 3, degrading and inhuman treatment is not applicable. The ICCPR covenant protects all persons likely to suffer torture as a result of refoulement, regardless of their conduct, nationality, or citizenship under Art 7 of this covenant.

Regardless of these conventions, and the CSR protection afforded to *de jure* refugees, the principle of non-refoulement within Art 33(1), it is argued, has become *Jus Cogens*[377].

## Articles Of Exclusion

The non-refoulement obligation does not attempt to address the possible conflict in rights between the obligation of the state, to refugees by the treaty, and the citizens of their own jurisdiction as a duty of care to its citizens. Furthermore, as can be seen from the wording of the definition, this does not discriminate between completely innocent refugees, at one end of a spectrum, and those who may have caused acts of terrorism, possibly seeking refugee protection to avoid prosecution; this is done by Art 1F of the convention:

> "The provisions of this Convention shall not apply to any person with respect to whom there are **serious reasons for considering** that:
>
> (a) he has **committed a crime against peace, a war crime, or a crime against humanity**, as defined in the international instruments drawn up to make provision in respect of such crimes;
>
> (b) he has **committed a serious non-political crime** outside the country of refuge prior to his admission to that country as a refugee;
>
> (c) he has been guilty of acts contrary to the purposes and principles of the United Nations."[378] *(Emphasis added)*

The burden of proof of these actions, only requires that the contracting state assessing the claim for protection should have, "serious reasons for considering", that one of the acts has been committed by the person, or that their involvement was sufficient to bring them within the purview of collusion to the act considered grounds for exclusion under Art 1F, no formal proof of penal prosecution is required, but the interpretation of the clauses therein are to be taken restrictively by the contracting state[379].

---

[377] Feller, Turk and Nicholson, 'Refugee Protection in International Law'
[378] The 1951 Convention Relating to the Status of Refugees and the 1967 Protocol

The application of Art 1F by states, has previously been used as a pre-emptory attempt to exclude those whom it has been deemed are unworthy of protection[379], a point with which it is easy to understand why the contracting state found it such an attractive a tool; this issue has now been clarified within the UNHCR guidance, and contracting states are reminded that all applications should be considered from the "standpoint of the inclusion clauses in the 1951 Convention"[381].

The guidance pays particular note to the fact that Art 1F & Arts 32 and 33(2) should not be confused as the giving the same effect, the latter two articles only concern the future risk that a recognised refugee may pose to the contracting state in the future[382].

## Application Of The Articles

This definition does nothing to limit the effect to those, who have protection from other competing conventions, such as the 1990 Convention on the Rights of the Child: This conflict is somewhat addressed in the guidance note[383] and the legislation; Section 55, of the Borders, Citizenship and Immigration Act 2009, which requires the UK competent authority making the assessment, to carry out their function in a way that takes into account the need to promote the welfare of children within the UK jurisdiction; the guidance states that caseworkers must not apply the actions set out in the guidance in regard to those Children affected by Art 1F, either directly, or as the children of those individuals covered under Art 1F[384]. Therefore, a child who may have committed an act under Art 1F, such as a child soldier, for example, would not be subject to refoulement under the legislation, nor would a terrorist's dependent family, they would need to establish a need for protection in their own right however[385]. This legislation and its commensurate guidance is a manifestation of the guidance from the UNHCR regarding this point[386].

---

[379] UNHCR, *Handbook and Guidelines on Procedures and Criteria for Determining Refugee Status* (2011)

[380] Hathaway JC and Harvey CJ, 'Framing Refugee Protection in the New World Disorder' (2001) 22 Immigr & Nat'lity L Rev 191

[381] UNHCR, *Handbook and Guidelines on Procedures and Criteria for Determining Refugee Status*

[382] Ibid

[383] Office H, *Immigration Rules Part 11* (2015)

[384] Ibid

[385] UNHCR *Handbook and Guidelines on Procedures and Criteria for Determining Refugee Status*

[386] UNHCR, *Guidelines on International Protection: Child Asylum Claims under Articles 1(a)2 and 1(F) of the 1951 Convention and/or 1967 Protocol Relating to the Status of Refugees* (2009)

Furthermore, these definitions do not address the issue of proximity to the activity which one might be excluded as the result of; if a *de facto* refugee has acquiesced to involvement to an act covered by Art 1F, by doing only as much as they feel they can, in order to not be subject to retribution by the group they are with, for example – the compulsion of necessity through duress; does that acquiescence make them culpable to the primary act?

The issue of complicity to the primary action, falling within the purview of Art 1F, was the issue at the heart of the case, JS (Sri Lanka) v UK: JS, a member of the Liberation Tigers of Tamil Eelam (LTTE) - also known as the Tamil Tigers - had been a senior member of the group within its intelligence division and had travelled to Colombo, Sri Lanka, as ordered. While in Colombo, it transpired that his identity and location had been discovered, and was likely to suffer persecution by the state, as a result; JS fled to the UK, and two days later applied for asylum.

JS' application for asylum was declined on the grounds of Art 1F(a), and 12(2)(a) of the Qualification Directive[387] as implemented by Regulation 2 and 7(1) of the Refugee or Person in Need of International Protection (Qualification) Regulations 2006 (SI 2006/2525). The question for the court was, how much involvement is required by a person seeking protection, for the exclusions of Art 1F to be applied to that individual? In citing the previous case of Gurung[388], the court refused to include the person who may have 'pulled the trigger'[389] for deserving of protection, but that "...even when complicity is established the assessment under Art 1F must take into account not only evidence about the status and level of the person in the organisation and factors such as duress and self-defence against superior orders as well as the availability of a moral choice"[390].

The court found that the appellant had not been a member of the LTTE during a period which it had sought to seek its political aims through the use of terrorism, although it had during other periods. Their lordships also expressed the opinion that the higher up in an organisation one is, the more likely that the individual might be culpable for action which they did not directly participate in[391]. The decision appears to follow the common law principle in tort, a field of law with which the English

---

[387] Council Directive 2004/83/Ec of 29 April 2004 on Minimum Standards for the Qualification and Status of Third Country Nationals or Stateless Persons as Refugees or as Persons Who Otherwise Need International Protection and the Content of the Protection Granted

[388] *Gurung V Secretary of State for the Home Department* Immigration Appeals Reports (IAT)

[389] *Js (Sri Lanka) V Uk*

[390] *Gurung V Secretary of State for the Home Department*

[391] *Js (Sri Lanka) V Uk*

judges would have found very comfortable, the liability for acts of third parties; if there was an unbroken chain of causation, *novus actus interveniens,* from the actions of the organisation, to the person claiming refugee protection, then that person will have sufficient proximity to the actions to be culpable for their commission[392].

Importantly, the court drew on various areas of international law, domestically, Art 30 and 25 of the ICC, Rome Statute[393] to define the *mens rea* and individual criminal responsibility, respectively, and the ICTY Statute[394], using Art 7(1) to identify individual criminal responsibility, and therefore proximity to the actions; using the definition of *mens rea* from the ICTY, Tadić case[395], Lord Brown, in the leading judgement, said that "when the accused is participating in (in the sense of assisting in or contributing to) a common plan or purpose, not necessarily to commit any specific or identifiable crime but to further the organisation's aims by committing article 1F crimes generally, no more need be established than that the accused had personal knowledge of such aims and intended to contribute to their commission"[396].

Resultantly, if culpability to actions under Art 1F, or Art 33(2) are established, the state can carry out one of three actions: i) Exclude the subject from protection and surrender for extradition to the requesting state of origin for prosecution; ii) Exclude from protection but grant humanitarian protection to the subject; iii) Grant refugee protection. However, it should be noted from a practical-political point of view, that to offer refugee or humanitarian protection to prevent refoulement to face torture, may satisfy lawyers, legal academics, and those mindful that human rights are for all, it is less likely to be seen as fair to the 'man on the Clapham omnibus'[397], and is regularly misappropriated to a government weakness[398] and has therefore, added 'fuel to the fire' against refugees in general and institutions seen as responsible for the oversight of the state's legal obligations.

---

[392] Cooke J, *Law of Tort* (Pearson Education 2003)
[393] Rome Statute of the International Criminal Court
[394] Updated Statute of the International Criminal Tribunal for the Former Yugoslavia
[395] *Prosecutor V. Dusko Tadic (Appeal Judgement)* International human rights reports
[396] *Js (Sri Lanka) V Uk*
[397] *Hall V Brooklands Auto-Racing Club [1933] 1 Kb 205* (Kings Bench Division, High Court)
[398] Furness H, 'Cost of Keeping Abu Qatada in Britain 'Tops £3m': The Cost of Keeping Radical Preacher Abu Qatada in Britain Has Risen to More Than £3 Million, It Has Been Claimed.' (2012) <http://www.telegraph.co.uk/news/uknews/defence/9251230/Cost-of-keeping-Abu-Qatada-in-Britain-tops-3m.html> accessed 22/04/2015

Regarding the choice of the state to expel; once the culpability of a crime, or ongoing behaviour, which falls within Art 1F or Art 33(2) is established, with due regard to Art 32, then the state is free expel that person, as this removes the non-refoulement protection of the convention; However, this does not diminish the effect of Art 3 of the ECHR, Art 3 of the CAT, or Art 7 of the ICCPR, nor the possibility that these treaties have become *Jus Cogens* law, and therefore the principle is applicable without the application of the treaties to torture applicable cases.

The Soering case[399] demonstrates this dilemma for the state: on one hand it is required to uphold the mechanism by which it is requested to submit a criminal suspect for trial by a sovereign nation, who have an extradition agreement with the UK; on the other hand the state is obligated to determine conditions in which the criminal suspect may be forced to endure, should they be extradited to the state requesting the arrest, and extradition to their territorial control. The implication for refugees seeking asylum are that, even those who may have engaged in acts subject to Art 1F exclusion, or that they might be involved in acts pursuant to Art 33(2) in the future, are given an absolute prohibition of transfer to a location that may torture, or impose degrading, or inhuman treatment upon that individual in question, such was the case of Chahal v UK[400].

Chahal, a Sikh activist while in India, and while he had lived in the UK; he had planned to assassinate the then Indian Prime Minister, Mr Rajiv Gandhi, during their visit to the UK; the previous Prime Minister, Mrs Indira Gandhi, it had been believed, had been assassinated by two members of her bodyguard team, who were of the Sikh faith[401].

Chahal was to be deported under the Immigration Act 1971 as he was not a British citizen, and as the Home Secretary had deemed his deportation was "conducive to the public good"[402].

The judgement came to the conclusion that the "Protection afforded by Art 3 is... wider than that provided by Art 32 – 33 of the Convention on the Status of Refugees"[403] and therefore, while Mr Chahal may have been subject to refoulement under the

---

[399] *Soering V. The United Kingdom* European Human Rights Reports (European Court of Human Rights)
[400] *Chahal V. United Kingdom* European Human Rights Reports
[401] Unknown, '1984: Indian Prime Minister Shot Dead' (Unknown) <http://news.bbc.co.uk/onthisday/hi/dates/stories/october/31/newsid_2464000/2464423.stm> accessed 19/04/2015
[402] *Chahal V Uk*
[403] Ibid

auspices of the CSR he could not be subject to mere possibility of a breach of Art 3 of the ECHR.

This latter point can be demonstrated in the case of Othman v UK: Perhaps better known as the UK's most notorious refugee of recent history, Abu Qatada, a Jordanian born cleric, who after fleeing Jordan on a forged UAE passport, claimed asylum in the UK during 1993. Although the courts did uphold his right to protection several times, the courts did outline what diplomatic assurances would be required in order to expel a person to a country that has previously been held to persecute a refugee within the meaning of the CSR. In order to gain diplomatic assurances sufficient for the ECHR Art 3, a state must show the following to the court, to which it will make its decision upon[404]:

1. Disclosure of the terms to the court
2. The specificity of the terms
3. The authority of the parties agreeing to the terms
4. The ability for a subordinate authority to derogate from the terms
5. The legality of the assured treatment, or the prohibition thereof in the transferring state
6. Whether the assurance has been given by a contracting state, or by a subordinate authority thereof
7. The length of time that the UK has had bilateral relations with the contracting state, and the quality of that relationship
8. Have the conditions of the assurances been objectively agreed with all the diplomatic parties and counsel for the person to be extradited
9. Is there an effective method for the protection from torture in the state receiving the person subject to the extradition
10. Any previous occurrences of ill-treatment to the subject by the contracting state
11. Has the reliability of the assurance been examined by the courts in both states

## Between A Rock And A Hard Place: Can't Extradite, Don't Want To Keep?

This would seem to give an option to the state in order to extradite someone subject to an extradition order, where they have committed an act under one of the Art 1F categories, or may do so under the Art 33(2) provision in the future; however,

---

[404] *Othman (Abu Qatada) V United Kingdom* Butterworths Human Rights Cases (European Court of Human Rights (Fourth Section))

for those who cannot be subject to refoulement due to the conditions imposed by the Othman case above, what can be done? One such option, or obligation is *Aut dedere aut judicare.*

In order to prosecute a crime committed extra-territorially, a court must establish competence of jurisdiction to hear the case; failure to establish this, may lead to an issue of the court not having jurisdiction, but the state being unable, or unwilling, to grant refugee status on the basis of the evidence[405]; a legal no-mans-land. The issue of jurisdiction, and the obligation to establish this, was the crux of the Belgium v Senegal case:

In the Belgium v Senegal case, regarding the failure of Senegal to prosecute or extradite, the former President of Chad, Hissène Habré, who was within their jurisdiction; the International Court of Justice held that, while the option of extradition was open to a state it was under an *erga omnes partes* obligation, that the obligation imposed upon the state was always to prosecute, where possible[406].

Where a person who has committed a crime outside the country of refuge, and a state has requested extradition, and this is unavailable, due to an Art 3 ECHR prohibition, for example, but this request would activate extradition proceedings otherwise; then an argument exists, that the state could, and should, assume universal jurisdiction under the passive personality principle; in the Universal Jurisdiction (Austria) case, the supreme court of Austria stated the following[407]:

> *"The extraditing State also has the right, in the cases where extradition for whatever reason is not possible, although according to the nature of the offence it would be permissible, to carry out a prosecution and impose punishment, instead of such action being taken by the requesting State."*

This again, was reaffirmed in the Hungarian Deserter case (Austria)[408] and it has been noted that fears of the refugee claimant escaping prosecution should not lead to refoulement being used, this principle is exercised by both Germany, and The Netherlands[409]; where an Art 1F case comes to light, then the refuge state is able to assume jurisdiction[410].

---

[405] Gilbert G and Rüsch AM, 'Jurisdictional Competence through Protection to What Extent Can States Prosecute the Prior Crimes of Those to Whom They Have Extended Refuge?' (2014) 12 Journal of International Criminal Justice 1093
[406] Ibid
[407] *Ogh Serie Strafsachen Xxix No. 32* International Law Reports (Supreme Court of Austria (Oberster Gerichtshof))
[408] *Hungarian Deserter (Austria) Case* International Law Reports (Supreme Court of Austria (Oberster Gerichtshof))

Commentators on the issue argue that if a state assumes the protective role from the state the person is fleeing, then that state, should also assume the jurisdiction of prior crimes carried out in the state in which they fled[411]; this would of course, would be conditional upon the acts being criminalised in both states prior to the act[412].

Where it is unpalatable to grant refugee, or humanitarian protection, for fear of providing succour to a person underserving of that protection, but that person cannot be returned to their state of origin due to the principle of non-refoulement, and that the refuge state is unable to gain a prosecution due to evidence, or simply a reluctance to prosecute, a fourth option could be desirable; the case could be referred, by the state, to the International Criminal Court for determination.

In addition to the state referring the case, the prosecutor for the ICC can act *proprio motu* and bring the case before the court themselves, if not referred by the United Nations Security Council[413]. While this principle is relatively new, it does have strong precedent from both the *ad hoc* tribunals, of the International Criminal Tribunal for Yugoslavia (ICTY), and the International Criminal Tribunal for Rwanda (ICTR), where both tribunals have constructed jurisdiction to enable them to proceed with cases that have questioned their competence to hear cases, the leading case in this regard is the case of Tadić.

Duško Tadić, A Serb from a small town in Bosnia, Kozarac[414], was indicted of crimes against humanity, grave breaches of the Geneva Conventions, and violations of the laws and customs of war against Bosnian Muslims; initially, Tadić argued that the tribunal did not have the jurisdictional competence to hear the case, and *inter alia* that the appeals chamber did not have the authority to hear an appeal on that point of law[415]. Among other specific questions, the appeals chamber asked itself, whether the Security Council had authority to constitute the tribunal at all; this was answered by referring to the UN Charter, Article 39, and the powers conferred to the Security

---

[409] Gilbert and Rüsch, 'Jurisdictional Competence through Protection to What Extent Can States Prosecute the Prior Crimes of Those to Whom They Have Extended Refuge?'
[410] Feller, Turk and Nicholson, 'Refugee Protection in International Law'
[411] Gilbert and Rüsch, 'Jurisdictional Competence through Protection to What Extent Can States Prosecute the Prior Crimes of Those to Whom They Have Extended Refuge?'
[412] Ibid
[413] Feller, Turk and Nicholson, 'Refugee Protection in International Law'
[414] Editorial, 'World: Europe Profile of a War Criminal ' (1999) <http://news.bbc.co.uk/1/hi/world/europe/515851.stm> accessed 21/04/2015
[415] *Prosecutor V. Dusko Tadic a/K/a "Dule"* - *Decision on the Defence Motion for Interlocutory Appeal on Jurisdiction* (International Criminal Tribunal for the former Yugoslavia (ICTY))

Council in the exercise to "maintain or restore international peace and security" were wide, although not unlimited, and the power to institute a tribunal was within the scope of the charter, and the role the appointed to tribunal had been set up to address the issue within the Article 39 remit specifically[416].

In a similar reasoning to the *ratio decidendi* of the Appeals chamber in Tadić; in the recent Al-Jedda case, the UNSC did not mention the issue of powers, as opposed to specifically granting them in Tadić, and had therefore, deliberately not given the powers that the UK argued were implicitly bestowed by virtue of UNSC resolution 1546; the ECtHR held that parties to the ECHR cannot intern civilians for non-criminal acts, unless there are explicit provisions for such action laid down in a Security Council resolution[417].

The International Criminal Court Act 2001 gave effect in domestic law to the Rome Statue, the International Criminal Court's founding statute; this was as the result of R v Jones and others, where the House of Lords found that only Parliament could make behaviour criminal and therefore legislating for it to be criminal[418]. The statute gives jurisdiction to the to the International Criminal Court for crimes which are defined within the act, pursuant to the treaty obligations within the Rome Statute - Crimes against humanity, war crimes and genocide. This is not as revolutionary as one may consider at a cursory glance when juxtaposed against decisions such as those claiming universal jurisdiction however, the decision in R v Jones and others, merely expressed the view that the court was not in the business of creating new offences, just that it provided judgements on the existing ones; the offences committed by persons pursuant to Art 1F could fit within the domestic criminal law of the UK, exercising their competence extra-territorially as is argued by Gilbert *et al*[419].

## Defence From Danger By Distance?

Schedule 3 of the Asylum and Immigration (Treatment of Claimants, etc) Act 2004, allows for the transfer of an asylum seeker to a third country in order for their claim to be processed, or for them to be granted refugee, or humanitarian protection by that state, in lieu of the United Kingdom. This allows the UK to have an asylum

---

[416] Ibid

[417] *Al-Jedda V United Kingdom* Butterworths Human Rights Cases (EUROPEAN COURT OF HUMAN RIGHTS (GRAND CHAMBER))

[418] *R V Jones and Others Ayliffe and Others V Director of Public Prosecutions Swain V Director of Public Prosecutions* United Kingdom House of Lords (House of Lords)

[419] Gilbert and Rüsch, 'Jurisdictional Competence through Protection to What Extent Can States Prosecute the Prior Crimes of Those to Whom They Have Extended Refuge?'

claim processed at arm's length from the UK, by the third-party state based on the principle within the Dublin II regulation, as part of the EU's Common European Asylum System (CEAS), which is based on the idea that an asylum seeker, who has entered the EU, should be processed by the first country which the asylum seeker was able to request refugee protection in[420].

This act also allows the implementation of one policy which has been mooted several times, as a panacea to, not only terrorists infiltrating borders, but the asylum issue in general, is the Extra-territorial processing, or Third-Country Processing (TCP), of those seeking refugee protection[421]; however, the Amnesty International report 2003 on the subject, highlighted the point that the asylum-seekers would "effectively be detained while their claims were assessed" and that "Diminished procedural safeguards envisaged in the UK New Vision would seriously undermine the fairness of procedures to which asylum-seekers would have access"[422].

Furthermore, it has been a matter of ongoing concern that one current example of this policy, in Australia particularly[423], has continued to find itself under the scrutiny of the Human Rights Council for this policy of Third-Country Processing of asylum-seekers, and that alternatives to the policy based in the territory of Australia should be found to replace the TCP policy[424].

The perceived treatment of persons at the hands of a state can, and does, contribute towards their reaction towards their host; if the person seeking refugee status perceives that the host state is maltreating them purposefully, then they could well be open to radicalisation; in effect, the treatment of potential refugees on the basis of preventing terrorism, could be a self-fulfilling prophecy[425].

---

[420] John-Hopkins M, 'The Emperor's New Safe Country Concepts: A Uk Perspective on Sacrificing Fairness on the Altar of Efficiency' (2009) International Journal of Refugee Law ; York S, 'Challenging 'Dublin'removals to Italy in the Uk Courts' (2010) 24 Journal of Immigration, Asylum and Nationality Law

[421] Garlick M, 'The Eu Discussions on Extraterritorial Processing: Solution or Conundrum?' (2006) 18 International Journal of Refugee Law 601; Kneebone S, McDowell C and Morrell G, 'A Mediterranean Solution? Chances of Success' ibid| Cited Pages492

[422] International A, *Uk/Eu/Unhcr: Unlawful and Unworkable - Extra-Territorial Processing of Asylum Claims.*, 2003)

[423] Although, the United States uses this method of Third-country Processing also.

[424] Council UHR, *Report of the Human Rights Council on Its 17th Session*, 2012)

[425] Driscoll B, 'Syrian Refugee Camps May Be a Breeding Ground for Terrorists, Says Malala Yousafzai' (*The Huffington Post*, 2014) <http://www.huffingtonpost.co.uk/2014/03/04/malala-yousafzai-syrian-refugee-camps-terrorism_n_4895670.html?1393946594&ncid=tweetlnkushpmg00000067> accessed 31/03/2015

Johan Steyn, Baron Steyn, remarked that "the type of justice meted out at Guantanamo Bay is likely to make martyrs of the prisoners in the moderate Muslim world with whom the west must work to ensure world peace and stability"[426], while this paper does not seek to suggest that the mere processing of refugees would necessarily amount to the same conditions faced by Guantanamo Bay detainees, it is all too easy to expect that large numbers of migrants and an underfunded, 'out-of-sight, out-of-mind', transit processing centre based away from Europe[427], could degenerate into the sort of conditions which were acquiesced by the British during the Boer War campaign concentration camps, which had originally been intended as refugee camps. The sort of lapses in basic hygiene and the resulting diseases, could all too soon lead to the migrants awaiting processing for refugee protection, to resent the situation they find themselves in.

This is an accusation levelled at the Australian model of keeping migrants at off-shore processing camps[428], which is already known for its rioting detainee population, due to their circumstances in which they are kept[429]. This treatment of migrants awaiting processing was justified by the Australian government by the 9/11 attacks[430], much in the same way the treatment of migrants has been justified by other governments subsequently to those attacks.

The Al-Jedda case emphasises the point that while the UK may not be the sovereign state in which a person is currently in, that the UK may be responsible for their welfare and well-being while the UK has effective control of their circumstances[431]. Would the UK be willing to use the powers under Schedule 3 of the Asylum and Immigration (Treatment of Claimants, etc) Act 2004, if it were not absolutely sure that the state sub-contracting the processing of those requesting

---

[426] Steyn J, 'Guantanamo Bay: The Legal Black Hole' (2004) 53 International and Comparative Law Quarterly 1

[427] Kneebone, McDowell and Morrell, 'A Mediterranean Solution? Chances of Success'

[428] Mathiesen K, "Even God Can't Help You Here': Nauru Refugees Describe a Life Devoid of Hope' *Guardian* (Thursday 19 March 2015)
<http://www.theguardian.com/world/2015/mar/19/even-god-cant-help-you-here-nauru-refugees-describe-a-life-devoid-of-hope> accessed 15/04/2015

[429] , 'Asylum Seekers Riot on Tiny Island of Nauru' *The Telegraph* (<http://www.telegraph.co.uk/news/worldnews/australiaandthepacific/nauru/10192187/Asylum-seekers-riot-on-tiny-island-of-Nauru.html> accessed 15/04/2015

[430] MP THPR, *Transcript of the Hon Peter Reith Mp Radio Interview with Derryn Hinch – 3ak* (2001)

[431] *Al-Jedda V Uk* ; Wagner A, 'Strasbourg Ruling May Change Uk's Responsibilities under the Human Rights Act' (*The Guardian*, 2011)
<http://www.theguardian.com/law/2011/jul/04/iraq-al-skeini-human-rights-act> accessed 1 December 2014

refugee protection would be given adequate treatment? Given the recent political events within the UK, the idea of the much-lambasted Australian system of Extra-territorial processing may gain traction within the UK[432].

This idea would need strict adherence to at least, the existing processing information details, such as EURODAC[433] – a system which has its own issues in of itself[434] – in order to select those persons which should be referred to prosecution for crimes under the remit of the Art 1F exclusions.

## Conclusion

It is clear that the issue of migration into, not only the UK, but the EU, is a pertinent problem; the UN states that since the beginning of the year, some 500 people have drowned while making the crossing from Libya to Italy, and around 8,000 people had been picked up in the 4 or so days between the Friday before a report from the BBC and the report itself[435].

This type of migration itself, helps to drive a narrative that there are two different kinds of migration, good and bad; that there are deserving migrants who should be given a form of protection[436], and those who should be driven back whence they came[437]. This again bleeds into the narrative that among the people fleeing for protection, there are some who would do the citizens of the UK harm[438], and has

---

[432] Marr D, 'Tony Abbott? He's Too Tough on Immigration for Me, Says Nigel Farage' (2015) <http://www.theguardian.com/australia-news/2015/apr/24/tony-abbott-hes-too-tough-on-immigration-for-me-says-nigel-farage> accessed 26/04/2015
[433] Commission E, *Eurodac Proposal: Completing the Common European Asylum System* (2012)
[434] Watch S, *Eu Fingerprinting by Force: Secret Discussions on "Systematic Identification" of Migrants and Asylum Seekers Including "Fingerprinting [with] the Use of a Proportionate Degree of Coercion" on "Vulnerable Persons, Such as Minors or Pregnant Women"*, 2015)
[435] Editorial, 'Libya Migrants: Hundreds Feared Drowned in Mediterranean' (2015) <http://www.bbc.co.uk/news/world-africa-32311358> accessed 16/04/2015
[436] Editorial, 'Nigel Farage Calls for Syrian Refugees to Be Allowed into Uk' (2013) <http://www.bbc.co.uk/news/uk-politics-25539843> accessed 25/04/2015
[437] Barrett D, 'Foreign Criminal Can Stay in Britain Because He Is an Alcoholic' (2015) <http://www.telegraph.co.uk/news/uknews/immigration/11565686/Foreign-criminal-can-stay-in-Britain-because-he-is-an-alcoholic.html> accessed 27/04/2015; Stone J, 'Katie Hopkins' Migrant 'Cockroaches' Column Resembles Pro-Genocide Propaganda, Says the Un' (2015) <http://www.independent.co.uk/news/uk/politics/katie-hopkins-migrant-cockroaches-column-resembles-progenocide-propaganda-says-the-un-10201959.html> accessed 25/04/2015
[438] PULLELLA P, 'Suspected Al-Qaeda Militants Arrested in Italy for Vatican Plot'

even been used as a threat by the states who feel that they are under pressure by those not taking their share of the burden[439]. However, there is little evidence that terrorist organisations are using that form of infiltration of their supporters to the EU, or the UK[440].

This public debate, of course, then leads the executive to over-react to criticism that they are simultaneously weak on terrorism and draconian on human rights, it being safer to err on the side of caution, than to allow an act of terrorism, the executive must be seen to be doing something, anything[441]. This rhetoric ignores the fact that the majority of extremism comes from those who have been born and lived in Britain all their lives and have been pushed towards extremist ideology by the same narrative that is directed at migrants, while being pulled away by that ideology that says that, that particular person can change things through acts of terror[442].

In this light, it may be true to say that the conflation of the two ideas - on one hand, migrants escaping persecution; on the other, terrorist's escaping prosecution, or worse still, infiltrating the UK to commit acts of terrorism - have meant that the British government has ceded to the rhetoric of the right-wing parties and the press, in general, that it is acceptable to impose erstwhile forbidden treatment upon those that do not have a vote, in favour of those that do.

Still, the point remains that the UK faces a problem of what to do with those who do not adhere to the moral values of the general British population at large and would want to wish harm upon the citizens of the UK. The narrative from the executive that they are unable to remove persons from the UK due to the ECHR, is somewhat inaccurate[443] and is no doubt aimed at the Conservative party's 1922 committee and their own voters, more than the wider public; dog-whistle politics[444],

---

(2015) <http://uk.reuters.com/article/2015/04/25/uk-italy-security-pakistan-idUKKBN0NF0DZ20150425> accessed 25/04/2015

[439] Waterfield B, 'Greece's Defence Minister Threatens to Send Migrants Including Jihadists to Western Europe' (2015) <http://www.telegraph.co.uk/news/worldnews/islamic-state/11459675/Greeces-defence-minister-threatens-to-send-migrants-including-jihadists-to-Western-Europe.html> accessed 25/04/2015

[440] Aliperta RAC, *The Flow of Illegal Immigrants across the Mediterranean* (2015)

[441] Holbrook J, 'How to Prevent Terrorism in Five Easy Steps!' (2015) <http://www.spiked-online.com/newsite/article/how-to-prevent-terrorism-in-five-easy-steps/16526#.VTvJoSFVhBc> accessed 25/04/2015

[442] FUREDI F, 'The Real Roots of Homegrown Terrorism' (2013) <http://www.spiked-online.com/newsite/article/13656#.VTvLhCFVhBc> accessed 25/04/2015

[443] Travis, 'Theresa May Criticises Human Rights Convention after Abu Qatada Affair'

which have, ironically given the subject, migrated to the UK to become part of the UK's mainstream political agenda, along with the Australian political strategist, Lynton Crosby[445]. As can be seen from the discussion in this paper, the government were able to extradite, on the conditions that the court set, which the executive then failed to meet initially[446].

Even where the executive was not able to gain effective diplomatic assurances, then there is precedent to affect jurisdiction over the case, the assumption of jurisdiction is an obligation in the case of crimes which fall within the remit of Art 1F. In the unlikely event that the UK could not provide competent jurisdiction, the executive can refer the case for prosecution at the International Criminal Court.

Finally, what is the solution to the issue of refugee protection obligations verses security? Preventing refugees coming to the UK would be unacceptable to the UNHCR, if not a gross demonstration of moral deficiency; could the potential refugees, currently using the surface route across the Sahara, from the sub-Saharan African countries, be held in camps in an amenable, and stable, North African country? Unlikely, these countries are currently either suffering internal struggles, or are not economically in a position to be in effective control[447]. The solution may lie in making the UNHCR responsible for the camp(s) and the processing of those claiming protection[448], with the economic support of the EU, and the agreement that the responsibility of giving protection is given to the EU member, and third-party states, in an equitable fashion based on their ability to absorb and support refugees effectively[449]. The administrative resources required would be tremendous; there would need to be access to data, such as EURODAC, as well intelligence from the police, military, and the security services of all 28 EU countries in order to identify those who may be guilty of acts pursuant to Art 1F, and the system would require

---

[444] *Dog-Whistle Politics* 2015)

[445] Beckett A, 'Lynton Crosby: Can the 'Lizard of Oz' Win the Election for the Conservatives?' (2015) <http://www.theguardian.com/politics/2015/mar/16/lynton-crosby-win-election-conservatives-tories-political-strategist> accessed 27/04/2015

[446] Editorial, 'Abu Qatada Case: Uk Agrees Assistance Treaty with Jordan' (*bbc.co.uk*, 2013) <http://www.bbc.co.uk/news/uk-22275000> accessed 9 December 2014

[447] Kneebone, McDowell and Morrell, 'A Mediterranean Solution? Chances of Success' ; O'Shea S, 'Mediterranean Migrant Crisis: Why Is No One Talking About Eritrea?' (2015) <http://www.theguardian.com/commentisfree/2015/apr/24/mediterranean-migrant-crisis-eritrea-western-allies?CMP=share_btn_fb> accessed 25/04/2015

[448] Garlick, 'The Eu Discussions on Extraterritorial Processing: Solution or Conundrum?'

[449] Kneebone S, McDowell C and Morrell G, 'A Mediterranean Solution? Chances of Success' ibid| Cited Pages492

regular inspection to ensure that the basic human rights of the asylum-seekers are being met, while they are waiting dissemination from the camp to ensure the issues which have arisen in other processing camps are averted before they arise. The issue regarding access to intelligence data, it should be mentioned, that this should only be done by the Europol, or similarly entrusted organisations, as the access to data by the third-party state, is a concern in itself, and that that data is only kept for so long as there is a legitimate need to do so[450].

The tools of providing security, while providing safety to those requesting refugee protection, are available within both the international legal framework, as well as the smaller regional framework within the EU, and these are further augmented by their incorporation within UK domestic legislation; the willingness to use the tools available does not seem to be apparent, but that is not the fault of the law, but those implementing it; justice is not served by exporting those persons who should be tried for their alleged crimes, when they can be tried in situ and provide an example to those whom may think that the UK is a safe haven for those who have committed crimes which deserve scrutiny by the courts.

Immigration control and security in regard to assessment of refugees for acts pursuant to Art 1F is a symbiotic relationship; if the southern European EU states are to implement systems such as EURODAC, which the northern European EU states benefit the greatest from, then the southern group must see that they are being treated fairly by the remainder of the EU[451]. If little, or no, cooperation is carried out in regard to EURODAC because of the rest of the Dublin regulations seem unfair to certain states, then the security aspect of knowing who is in the EU, and resultantly

---

[450] UNHCR, 'Un High Commissioner for Refugees (Unhcr), an Efficient and Protective Eurodac - Unhcr Comments on the Commission's Amended Proposal for a Regulation of the European Parliament and of the Council on the Establishment of 'Eurodac' for the Comparison of Fingerprints for the Effective Application of Regulation (Eu) No [.../...] (Establishing the Criteria and Mechanisms for Determining the Member State Responsible for Examining an Application for International Protection Lodged in One of the Member States by a Third-Country National or a Stateless Person) and to Request Comparisons with Eurodac Data by Member States' Law Enforcement Authorities and Europol for Law Enforcement Purposes and Amending Regulation (Eu) No 1077/2011 Establishing a European Agency for the Operational Management of Large-Scale It Systems in the Area of Freedom, Security and Justice (Recast Version)' (2012)
<http://www.refworld.org/docid/50ad01b72.html> accessed 29/04/2015
[451] Marszal JHaA, 'Angela Merkel Calls for New Rules for Distributing Asylum Seekers in Europe' (2015)
<http://www.telegraph.co.uk/news/worldnews/europe/germany/11561430/Angela-Merkel-calls-for-new-rules-for-distributing-asylum-seekers-in-Europe.html> accessed 29/04/2015

the UK, is made difficult, this also makes it easier for potential refugees to 'drop through the cracks'.

The balancing act of providing security, while acknowledging the UK's responsibility within International Refugee Law, is not an intractable problem; however, it is not one which can be carried out as a sovereign nation alone, however; the problem must be tackled regionally as a member of a larger group, and in doing so, the UK may have to cede power to that larger group, of the EU, in order to maintain collective security for all of the states within the region of Europe; making any possible solution something which may be more easily sold regionally within the EU, than it is domestically.

# References

Cooke J, Law of Tort (Pearson Education 2003)

Hall V Brooklands Auto-Racing Club [1933] 1 Kb 205 (Kings Bench Division, High Court)

Ogh Serie Strafsachen Xxix No. 32 International Law Reports (Supreme Court of Austria (Oberster Gerichtshof))

Hungarian Deserter (Austria) Case International Law Reports (Supreme Court of Austria (Oberster Gerichtshof))

Soering V. The United Kingdom European Human Rights Reports (European Court of Human Rights)

Prosecutor V. Dusko Tadic (Appeal Judgement) International human rights reports

Prosecutor V. Dusko Tadic a/K/a "Dule" - Decision on the Defence Motion for Interlocutory Appeal on Jurisdiction (International Criminal Tribunal for the former Yugoslavia (ICTY))

Chahal V. United Kingdom European Human Rights Reports

Gurung V Secretary of State for the Home Department Immigration Appeals Reports (IAT)

R V Jones and Others Ayliffe and Others V Director of Public Prosecutions Swain V Director of Public Prosecutions United Kingdom House of Lords (House of Lords)

R (on the Application of Js) (Sri Lanka) (Respondent) V Secretary of State for the Home Department (Appellant) United Kingdom Supreme Court Reports (Supreme Court)

Al-Jedda V United Kingdom Butterworths Human Rights Cases (EUROPEAN COURT OF HUMAN RIGHTS (GRAND CHAMBER))

Othman (Abu Qatada) V United Kingdom Butterworths Human Rights Cases (European Court of Human Rights (Fourth Section))

Dog-Whistle Politics 2015)

Aliperta RAC, The Flow of Illegal Immigrants across the Mediterranean (2015)

UNHCR, Guidelines on International Protection: Child Asylum Claims under Articles 1(a)2 and 1(F) of the 1951 Convention and/or 1967 Protocol Relating to the Status of Refugees (2009)

UNHCR, Handbook and Guidelines on Procedures and Criteria for Determining Refugee Status (2011)

MP THPR, Transcript of the Hon Peter Reith Mp Radio Interview with Derryn Hinch – 3ak (2001)

Feller E, Turk V and Nicholson F, 'Refugee Protection in International Law' (2003) UNHCR's Global Consultations on International Protection

Garlick M, 'The Eu Discussions on Extraterritorial Processing: Solution or Conundrum?' (2006) 18 International Journal of Refugee Law 601

Gilbert G and Rüsch AM, 'Jurisdictional Competence through Protection to What Extent Can States Prosecute the Prior Crimes of Those to Whom They Have Extended Refuge?' (2014) 12 Journal of International Criminal Justice 1093

Hathaway JC and Harvey CJ, 'Framing Refugee Protection in the New World Disorder' (2001) 22 Immigr & Nat'lity L Rev 191

John-Hopkins M, 'The Emperor's New Safe Country Concepts: A Uk Perspective on Sacrificing Fairness on the Altar of Efficiency' (2009) International Journal of Refugee Law

Kneebone S, McDowell C and Morrell G, 'A Mediterranean Solution? Chances of Success' (2006) 18 International Journal of Refugee Law 492

Steyn J, 'Guantanamo Bay: The Legal Black Hole' (2004) 53 International and Comparative Law Quarterly 1

York S, 'Challenging 'Dublin'removals to Italy in the Uk Courts' (2010) 24 Journal of Immigration, Asylum and Nationality Law

Office H, Immigration Rules Part 11 (2015)

, 'Asylum Seekers Riot on Tiny Island of Nauru' The Telegraph (<http://www.telegraph.co.uk/news/worldnews/australiaandthepacific/nauru/10192187/Asylum-seekers-riot-on-tiny-island-of-Nauru.html> accessed 15/04/2015

Mathiesen K, ''Even God Can't Help You Here': Nauru Refugees Describe a Life Devoid of Hope' Guardian (Thursday 19 March 2015) <http://www.theguardian.com/world/2015/mar/19/even-god-cant-help-you-here-nauru-refugees-describe-a-life-devoid-of-hope> accessed 15/04/2015

Commission E, Eurodac Proposal: Completing the Common European Asylum System (2012)

Council UHR, Report of the Human Rights Council on Its 17th Session, 2012)

ECRE, Ecre Comments on Regulation (Eu) No 604/2013 of the European Parliament and of the Council of 26 June 2013 Establishing the Criteria and Mechanisms for Determining the Member State Responsible for Examining an Application for International Protection Lodged in One of the Member States by a Third-Country National or a Stateless Person (Recast). 2015)

International A, Uk/Eu/Unhcr: Unlawful and Unworkable - Extra-Territorial Processing of Asylum Claims., 2003)

UNHCR, Un High Commissioner for Refugees (UNHCR), UNHCR Comments on the European Commission's Proposal for a Recast of the Regulation of the European Parliament and of the Council Establishing the Criteria and Mechanisms for Determining the Member State Responsible for Examining an Application for International Protection Lodged in One of the Member States by a Third Country

National or a Stateless Person ("Dublin II") (Com(2008) 820, 3 December 2008) and the European Commission's Proposal for a Recast of the Regulation of the European Parliament and of the Council Concerning the Establishment of 'Eurodac' for the Comparison of Fingerprints for the Effective Application of [the Dublin II Regulation] (Com(2008) 825, 3 December 2008), 2009)

Watch S, EU Fingerprinting by Force: Secret Discussions on "Systematic Identification" of Migrants and Asylum Seekers Including "Fingerprinting [with] the Use of a Proportionate Degree of Coercion" on "Vulnerable Persons, Such as Minors or Pregnant Women", 2015)

The 1951 Convention Relating to the Status of Refugees and the 1967 Protocol

Rome Statute of the International Criminal Court

Council Directive 2004/83/Ec of 29 April 2004 on Minimum Standards for the Qualification and Status of Third Country Nationals or Stateless Persons as Refugees or as Persons Who Otherwise Need International Protection and the Content of the Protection Granted

Updated Statute of the International Criminal Tribunal for the Former Yugoslavia

Barrett D, 'Foreign Criminal Can Stay in Britain Because He Is an Alcoholic' (2015) <http://www.telegraph.co.uk/news/uknews/immigration/11565686/Foreign-criminal-can-stay-in-Britain-because-he-is-an-alcoholic.html> accessed 27/04/2015

Beckett A, 'Lynton Crosby: Can the 'Lizard of Oz' Win the Election for the Conservatives?' (2015) <http://www.theguardian.com/politics/2015/mar/16/lynton-crosby-win-election-conservatives-tories-political-strategist> accessed 27/04/2015

Driscoll B, 'Syrian Refugee Camps May Be a Breeding Ground for Terrorists, Says Malala Yousafzai' (The Huffington Post, 2014) <http://www.huffingtonpost.co.uk/2014/03/04/malala-yousafzai-syrian-refugee-camps-terrorism_n_4895670.html?1393946594&ncid=tweetlnkushpmg00000067> accessed 31/03/2015

Editorial, 'World: Europe Profile of a War Criminal ' (1999) <http://news.bbc.co.uk/1/hi/world/europe/515851.stm> accessed 21/04/2015

Editorial, 'Abu Qatada Awarded Compensation by European Judges for 'Breach of Human Rights'' (Telegraph, 2009) <http://www.telegraph.co.uk/news/uknews/4696480/Abu-Qatada-awarded-compensation-by-European-judges-for-breach-of-human-rights.html> accessed 9 December 2014

Editorial, 'Abu Qatada Case: Uk Agrees Assistance Treaty with Jordan' (bbc.co.uk, 2013) <http://www.bbc.co.uk/news/uk-22275000> accessed 9 December 2014

Editorial, 'Nigel Farage Calls for Syrian Refugees to Be Allowed into Uk' (2013) <http://www.bbc.co.uk/news/uk-politics-25539843> accessed 25/04/2015

Editorial, 'Libya Migrants: Hundreds Feared Drowned in Mediterranean' (2015) <http://www.bbc.co.uk/news/world-africa-32311358> accessed 16/04/2015

FUREDI F, 'The Real Roots of Homegrown Terrorism' (2013) <http://www.spiked-online.com/newsite/article/13656#.VTvLhCFVhBc> accessed 25/04/2015

Furness H, 'Cost of Keeping Abu Qatada in Britain 'Tops £3m': The Cost of Keeping Radical Preacher Abu Qatada in Britain Has Risen to More Than £3 Million, It Has Been Claimed.' (2012) <http://www.telegraph.co.uk/news/uknews/defence/9251230/Cost-of-keeping-Abu-Qatada-in-Britain-tops-3m.html> accessed 22/04/2015

Holbrook J, 'How to Prevent Terrorism in Five Easy Steps!' (2015) <http://www.spiked-online.com/newsite/article/how-to-prevent-terrorism-in-five-easy-steps/16526#.VTvJoSFVhBc> accessed 25/04/2015

Marr D, 'Tony Abbott? He's Too Tough on Immigration for Me, Says Nigel Farage' (2015) <http://www.theguardian.com/australia-news/2015/apr/24/tony-abbott-hes-too-tough-on-immigration-for-me-says-nigel-farage> accessed 26/04/2015

Marszal JHaA, 'Angela Merkel Calls for New Rules for Distributing Asylum Seekers in Europe' (2015) <http://www.telegraph.co.uk/news/worldnews/europe/germany/11561430/Angela-Merkel-calls-for-new-rules-for-distributing-asylum-seekers-in-Europe.html> accessed 29/04/2015

O'Shea S, 'Mediterranean Migrant Crisis: Why Is No One Talking About Eritrea?' (2015) <http://www.theguardian.com/commentisfree/2015/apr/24/mediterranean-migrant-crisis-eritrea-western-allies?CMP=share_btn_fb> accessed 25/04/2015

PULLELLA P, 'Suspected Al-Qaeda Militants Arrested in Italy for Vatican Plot' (2015) <http://uk.reuters.com/article/2015/04/25/uk-italy-security-pakistan-idUKKBN0NF0DZ20150425> accessed 25/04/2015

Stone J, 'Katie Hopkins' Migrant 'Cockroaches' Column Resembles Pro-Genocide Propaganda, Says the Un' (2015) <http://www.independent.co.uk/news/uk/politics/katie-hopkins-migrant-cockroaches-column-resembles-progenocide-propaganda-says-the-un-10201959.html> accessed 25/04/2015

Travis A, 'Theresa May Criticises Human Rights Convention after Abu Qatada Affair' (2013) <http://www.theguardian.com/world/2013/jul/08/theresa-may-human-rights-abu-qatada> accessed 23/04/2015

UNHCR, 'Un High Commissioner for Refugees (UNHCR), an Efficient and Protective Eurodac - Unhcr Comments on the Commission's Amended Proposal for a Regulation of the European Parliament and of the Council on the Establishment of 'Eurodac' for the Comparison of Fingerprints for the Effective Application of Regulation (Eu) No [.../...] (Establishing the Criteria and Mechanisms for Determining the Member State Responsible for Examining an Application for International Protection Lodged in One of the Member States by a Third-Country National or a Stateless Person) and to Request Comparisons with Eurodac Data by Member States' Law Enforcement Authorities and Europol for Law Enforcement Purposes and Amending Regulation (Eu) No 1077/2011 Establishing a European

Agency for the Operational Management of Large-Scale It Systems in the Area of Freedom, Security and Justice (Recast Version)' (2012) <http://www.refworld.org/docid/50ad01b72.html> accessed 29/04/2015

Unknown, '1984: Indian Prime Minister Shot Dead' (Unknown) <http://news.bbc.co.uk/onthisday/hi/dates/stories/october/31/newsid_2464000/2464423.stm> accessed 19/04/2015

Wagner A, 'Strasbourg Ruling May Change Uk's Responsibilities under the Human Rights Act' (The Guardian, 2011) <http://www.theguardian.com/law/2011/jul/04/iraq-al-skeini-human-rights-act> accessed 1 December 2014

Waterfield B, 'Greece's Defence Minister Threatens to Send Migrants Including Jihadists to Western Europe' (2015) <http://www.telegraph.co.uk/news/worldnews/islamic-state/11459675/Greeces-defence-minister-threatens-to-send-migrants-including-jihadists-to-Western-Europe.html> accessed 25/04/2015

# Index

1648 Peace of Westphalia ................. 63

1948 Universal Declaration of Human Rights ............................................... 65

1948 Universal Declaration of Human Rights (UDHR) ................................... 27

1949 Fourth Geneva Convention Relative to the Protection of Civilian Persons in time of War .................. 30

1951 Convention on the Status of Refugees ..................................... 25, 75

1951 Convention on the Status of the Refugee ............................................ 78

1951 United Nations Convention Relating to the Status of Refugees, and the 1967 Protocol .................. 2, 5

1965 International Convention on the Elimination of All Forms of Racial Discrimination (ICERD) ................ 28

1966 International Convention on Civil and Political Rights (ICCPR). 28

1966 International Covenant on Economic, Social and Cultural Rights (ICESCR) ............................ 28

1969 Convention Governing the Specific Aspects of Refugee Problems in Africa ......................... 61

1969 Organisation of African Unity Convention Governing the Specific Aspects of Refugee Problems in Africa ................................................. 78

1969 Organization of African Unity (OAU) .................................................. 5

1979 Convention on the Elimination of All Forms of Discrimination against Women (CEDAW) .............. 28

1984 Cartagena Declaration .............. 61

1984 Convention against Torture and Other Cruel, Inhuman or Degrading Treatment or Punishment (CAT) 28, 122

1989 Convention on the Rights of the Child (CRC) ...................................... 28

1990 Convention on the Rights of the Child ................................................ 123

Afghanistan ........................................... 7

Ahmed v Australia ............................. 39

Al Qaeda ............................................. 19

Al-Jedda case ................................... 133

Anti-Terrorism, Crime and Security Act 2001 ............................................ 36

Art 1F - Convention on the Status of Refugees ........................................ 122

Asylum seeker ..................................... 2

Asymmetric warfare .......................... 17

Attitudes towards racial groups and refugees ............................................ 36

Australia ................. 4, 17, 35, 48, 76, 81

*Aut dedere aut judicare* .................... 128

Belgium v Senegal ........................... 128

Benefit of Refugees ............................. 9

Borders, Citizenship and Immigration Act 2009 .......................................... 123

Brexit ..................................................... 7

Cessation of the Application of the Law on the Use of Abandoned Property ......................................... 101

Chahal v UK ..................................... 126

Čolić and Others v. Bosnia and Herzegovina ................................... 106

Commission for Real Property Claims of Displaced Persons and Refugees ........................................102

Common European Asylum System (CEAS)..............................................131

Convention Governing the Specific Aspects of Refugee Problems in Africa (OAU Convention of 1969)....5

Convention Plus strategy ...................41

Conventions protecting refugees .....79

Covenant between the state and terrorist ..........................................18

Dabaab refugee camp........................21

*De facto* refugees ...............................1

*De Jure* refugees.................................2

Department of International Protection (DIP)..............................33

Destruction and expropriation of property..........................................93

dog-whistle politics.........................135

Đokić v. Bosnia and Herzegovina ...104

Dublin convention ....................5, 6, 88

Enforcement of refugee rights .........37

Ethnic cleansing..........................18, 102

European Court of Human Rights 39, 104, 120

Executive Committee of the High Commissioner's Programme (EXCOM)..........................................33

Expulsion and Extradition................26

General Framework Agreement for Peace Annex 7 ...............................100

Genocide...............................................18

Globalisation................................16, 17

Greece ....................................................5

Human Rights Council .....................38

Illegal immigrant ...............................84

Individual rights vs Collective rights ..........................................................31

Inherent problems in the West..........9

Internally Displaced Persons .3, 75, 94

International Criminal Court Act 2001 ........................................................130

Italy......................................................87

JS (Sri Lanka) v UK...................120, 124

Kenya ............................................14, 24

Land, property and other possessions ..........................................................93

Law on Cessation of the Application of the Law on Temporarily Abandoned Real Property Owned by Citizens........................................101

Law on the Cessation of the Application of the Law on Abandoned Apartments................101

Liberation Tigers of Tamil Eelam (LTTE) .......................................40, 124

Lynton Crosby..................................135

Migration Amendment (Excision from Migration Zone) Act 2001.....81

*Mujahedeen* ..........................................7

Multiculturalism ................................17

MV Tampa....................................35, 81

Nauru ..................................35, 133, 139

Negative narratives ............................7

New Zealand......................................35

Non-refoulement 3, 28, 34, 40, 87, 122, 126, 129

Office of the High Representative ..102

Othman v UK....................................127

Palestine refugees................................3

PATRIOT Act 2001 .................................. 36
Peacebuilding ...................................... 107
People in refugee-like situations ....... 2
Proxy war ............................................. 20
R v Jones ............................................. 131
Radicalisation .............................. 10, 132
Refoule ........................................... 35, 42
Refugee definition ...................... 51, 58
Refugees seeking asylum in the EU . 83
Restitution .......................................... 110
Right to return .................................... 95
Rule of law ......................................... 108
Rwanda ............................................... 111
Safe third countries ........................... 88
*Sale v. Haitian Centers Council* case .... 88
Soering case ............................... 39, 126
Sovereignty ... 25, 32, 41, 50, 59, 65, 76
State as the monopoly user of force . 16

Suresh case ......................................... 40
Syria ..................................................... 75
Tadić case ................................... 125, 130
The Bosnian war ................................. 18
Third-Country Processing (TCP) .... 131
Treaty of Westphalia 1648 ................. 50
UNHCR ............................. 3, 33, 37, 123
United Kingdom .................................. 6
United Nations Relief and Works Agency for Palestine Refugees in the Near East (UNRWA) ................... 3
United States ............................... 35, 59
Universal Declaration of Human Rights ........................................... 27, 28
Universal Jurisdiction (Austria) case .......................................................... 129
UNSC resolution 1031 ........................ 97
Voluntary return of migrants ........... 10
Weapons of Mass Destruction .......... 20

Printed in Great Britain
by Amazon